Nov. 19. 2017

Dear Gilles

Hope you like your gift & Have a wonderful Birthday

Love

Bernie & Suzanne ♡♡

xox

150 YEARS OF
CANADIAN
BEER LABELS

LAWRENCE C. SHERK

TouchWood
Editions

To the many people who built Canada's brewing business over the last centuries, and to the hundreds involved in Canada's growing craft beer industry today.

FOREWORD

"Ask Larry."

I don't know how many times I heard those words when I was getting to work on my first beer book, *Brew North* (Greystone Books, 2010). My dream was to fill the book with lots of pictures of old bottle caps, ads, and, of course, labels—all those neat doodads and gewgaws typically labelled "breweriana." But whenever I'd meet collectors and tell them what I was interested in, I'd get the same answer: "Ask Larry." Or some variant of it: "You should see what Larry has." "I don't have anything that Larry doesn't."

I'd heard about Larry Sherk, and had assumed he was just one collector among many. But, as I realized the day I first crossed the threshold of his small row house in Toronto's east end, there is only one Larry Sherk. Larry is collector zero, the first-ever guy, way back in the 1970s, to think that the detritus of Canada's long beer history was something worth collecting and preserving. The story was he'd started with a few beer trays and just kept going. By the time I visited him there were more than thirty on the walls (that wasn't all of them, either), shelves lined with commemorative glasses, drawers filled with bottle openers and binders—so many binders!—bulging with plastic sleeves filled with coasters and labels.

Those binders told me something: this wasn't the work of a guy who squirrels away forty years of newspapers in his house, sticking them wherever there was a spare square inch of floor space. No, Larry knew what he had and where it was. What's more, as I learned as we started sifting through his collection looking for what might work in my book, he could tell you about it. I'd hold up a stubby bearing the label of a brewery I had never heard of, and Larry could tell me when and where it had launched and what had happened to it. He was more than a collector: he was a repository of history, but a history that, like the objects he collected, often got overlooked. A lot of what Larry told me went into my book, and when I wanted someone to read it for historical accuracy, Larry was the person I chose.

I also learned that Larry likes to share. It was in that spirit a few years ago that he donated the bulk of his label collection to the Thomas Fisher Rare Book Library at the University of Toronto, where it will be preserved and available for a long time to come for anyone interested in it. Knowing Larry, I'd say that's the spirit behind this book, too.

Looking at the labels Larry has gathered here is like taking a visual journey through history. They will teach you a lot. The first ones are pretty primitive—just printed circles, really. Then, as time marches on, they begin to grow progressively more elaborate, as seen in the multicoloured images. By the 1960s they come under the sway of modernist minimalism and make more use of metallic stamping. Taken individually (and as a whole), these labels are like little lessons in the evolution of printing and graphic design. What they depict is great, too—a sort of visual shorthand. If it's a lager, it's a safe bet there will be a jolly Bavarian with a stein, and a bock pretty much demands a goat or a happy friar, perhaps both. Others are self-consciously Canadian: mighty waterfalls, a beaver or a proud moose, the image of Samuel de Champlain, or—my all-time favourite—the Fathers of Confederation busily at work creating Canada, as seen on the label of the Saskatoon Brewing Company's '67 Beer. There's a melancholy quality to the labels, too: Dawes, Dow, Sicks'—they bear the names of so many breweries that vanished during the consolidation of Canadian brewing in the twentieth century into fewer and fewer hands. Thanks to the craft beer revolution, Canadian beer is in great shape today, but it is still sad to be reminded of all we've lost.

What Larry has put together here is a great gift to beer fans and Canadians from coast to coast. So crack open your favourite craft beer—one with a terrific label—pull up a chair, and take a deep, long drink of *150 Years of Canadian Beer Labels*.

IAN COUTTS

INTRODUCTION

I've said it before, and I'll say it again: the story of beer is the story of Canada.

The art of labelling beer bottles dates back to the 1840s in England, when Bass & Company had a label produced for their bottles of East India Pale Ale. By 1855 more breweries in Great Britain were using labels on their bottles. In Canada, the first labels are from the 1850s and appeared on bottles of Molson's beers, and on the bottles of Grant, Middlewood & Townsend (in Hamilton, Ontario). Examples of the early Molson labels are in the Molson Archives, which are in the National Archives of Canada.

Early labels in this book are from my collection, which is now at the Fisher Rare Book Library at the University of Toronto. These include the two Dow labels from the late 1870s and the Labatt label from 1889.

Labelling of beer bottles spread rapidly in Eastern Canada in the second half of the nineteenth century, and subsequent to this as breweries were established in Western Canada. Some early pre-Prohibition labels were quite simple—as seen, for example, on Orillia Brewing & Malting's XX Porter, while early Labatt's labels displayed more complex designs. Many labels often featured medals to boast of the awards won in competitions in the United States and Europe; others had illustrations of their breweries while employing some artistic license when it came to depicting the size of their breweries.

Prohibition came to Canada during WWI; it ended after the war, province by province, starting in 1921 in Quebec, BC, and the Yukon and finally ending in PEI in 1948. Many breweries closed and didn't reopen after Prohibition, but some kept open, producing beverages with an alcohol content of less than 2.5 % proof spirits. Many labels from this period can be dated by the percentages indicated on them.

Ontario had the largest number of operating breweries after Prohibition, but consolidation started in 1930 in Ontario, and soon spread across the country, leading to the elimination of many of these brands, while some local brands were kept by the national brewers.

The 1980s saw the opening of the first new and local microbreweries and brewpubs in BC and Ontario. The 1990s and the twenty-first century has seen the rapid opening and growth of new "craft" breweries, both microbreweries and brewpubs with modern purity methods. Their craft labels are often quite artistic and colourful.

I've been asked how many labels are in my collection. The answer is that I really have no idea. Unlike some collectors, I've never kept track. What I *can* tell you is that it numbers over 20,000, and that number grows weekly as I acquire labels from Canada's many burgeoning craft breweries.

When putting this book together, I was presented with the immense task of choosing a relatively small number of labels to share with you. If it had been possible to feature every single brewery, large and small, across Canada, I would have happily done so without hesitation. What I am able to offer you, to the best of my ability, is a sampling of my collection at the Fisher Rare Book Library, with a cross-section of labels that span the decades and provinces, giving equal exposure to independent breweries as well as the larger ones.

I find it encouraging that there are emerging breweries and label designers today who, through their amazing creativity and diversity in label design, are reviving and advancing a long-standing tradition in new and inspiring ways. Because of this, we can look forward to the continuing story of Canada, as told through this distinct medium, for many years to come.

WILLIAM DOW & COMPANY
Montreal, Quebec

WILLIAM DOW MILD ALE XX
WILLIAM DOW STRONG ALE XXX

Late 1870s

The Dow Brewery traces itself back to 1790. However, William Dow did not join the brewery until 1829. These two Dow labels—found at a nostalgia show in Woodstock, Ontario—are the earliest in my collection, now housed at the Thomas Fisher Rare Book Library at the University of Toronto, and date from the late 1870s. Other Dow labels from this era were featured in the February 2, 1878 issue of *Canadian Illustrated News*; newspapers at this time typically used images of beer labels when advertising various brands.

LABATT & COMPANY
London, Ontario

INDIA PALE ALE

1889

In 1847, John Labatt acquired interest in a London brewery that started in 1828. Since then it has grown into one of Canada's two nationwide brewing companies, with breweries spanning the country from Newfoundland to British Columbia.

This label matches one in a Labatt's ad in an 1889 copy of the novel *Commodore Junk*, published in London, Ontario, which also features an ad for Carling Brewing & Malting Co, with illustrations for Carling's Amber Ale and Porter "kept by all leading grocers in Canada."

KUNTZ EXPORT LAGER BEER

Circa 1890

Founded in 1840 by David Kuntz, The Kuntz Brewery Limited was an early brewer of lager beer in Canada. Louie Kuntz, David's son, renamed it the Park Brewery, which was in operation from 1884 to 1901. F. Bauer was manager from 1891 to 1895, dating this label to that period. The elegant, flowing script is a superb example of the design aesthetic of that era.

E K E R S ' B R E W E R Y
Montreal, Quebec

AMBER ALE

Late 1890s

In 1891, this brewery was established as the Canadian Brewing Company; the company name was changed to Canadian Breweries Limited in 1899 when it merged with the Ekers' Brewery. The Ekers name continued on their beers until 1930. On this label, we see the signature of Henry Archer Ekers (the twenty-eighth mayor of Montreal, in office between 1906 and 1908), who ran the brewery from 1885 to 1899. The design is a good representation of Quebec labels of that era.

THE CANADIAN BREWERIES LIMITED

EKERS' BREWERY

H.A. Ekers

Registered   Trade Mark

AMBER ALE

BOTTLED AT THE BREWERY

MONTREAL

SUCCESSORS TO EKERS' BREWERY

PEMBROKE BREWING COMPANY
Pembroke, Ontario

XXX PORTER

1890s

Established by Frank X. Mattman, who ran it with George Jamieson and C. Buege, the Pembroke Brewing Company was a short-lived brewery that operated only from 1890 to 1895. Situated a mile outside of town, it was destroyed by fire in early 1895. Although it was operated in a new building, it was not covered by insurance and, unfortunately, was never rebuilt.

NOTICE:
TO HAVE THIS PORTER IN
FINE CONDITION THE BOTTLE
SHOULD REMAIN UPRIGHT FOR
24 HOURS AND CONTENTS
CAREFULLY DECANTED
WITHOUT SHAKING.

PEMBROKE BREWING CO
PORTER
XXX
PEMBROKE.

PRESCOTT BREWING & MALTING COMPANY
Prescott, Ontario

XXX PORTER

1890s

This brewery operated under the name Prescott Brewing & Malting Company from 1871 to 1901, but was originally founded in 1857. It was operated by members of the Labatt family from London, Ontario, from 1865 to 1871.

This colourful label dates from the late 1890s and features a medal won in the Colonial and Indian Exhibition, held in London, England, in 1896. Another one of the medals commemorates the landing of Columbus; yet another proclaims Albert Edward, Prince of Wales, as the executive president of the Colonial and Indian Exhibition.

SUPERIOR BREWING AND MALTING COMPANY
Port Arthur, Ontario

DIAMOND BEER

1899

This brewery can be traced back to 1876, and became known as the Superior Brewing and Malting Company in 1899. It operated under this name until 1913, when it assumed the name of its beer and became the Diamond Brewery Limited. It was eventually acquired by Doran's and closed in 1994.

SUPERIOR BREWING AND MALTING CO.

DIAMOND BEER

PORT ARTHUR, ONT.

DAVIES BREWING & MALTING COMPANY
Toronto, Ontario

DAVIES' XXX PORTER

1900

The Don Brewery was established in 1844 beside the Don River. Taken over by Thomas Davies Sr. in 1849, it was known as the Davies Brewing & Malting Company from 1883 to 1901. Thomas Davies Jr. sold it to a British syndicate in late 1900. It reopened under a new name—Davies Brewing Company—but was seriously damaged by fire in 1907. Part of the brewery still stands today, and has been redeveloped into condominiums. Here we have a complex yet subtle style of label typical of the stone lithography—as crafted by Barkley, Clark & Co., lithographers in Toronto—used at that time.

JAMES READY LIMITED
Saint John, New Brunswick

READY'S LAGER BEER

Early 1900s

In 1867, James Ready established his brewery in Saint John and operated it under the name James Ready Limited until 1905 when he added the name New Brunswick Brewery. These two names were used until 1913 when the company was incorporated as Ready's Breweries Limited. Today it is the home of the Moosehead Breweries Limited of Saint John, New Brunswick, in what was the Fairville suburb before becoming part of Saint John in 1957. On this label we see that James Ready made good use of his name, initials, and signature.

DOMINION BREWERY COMPANY
Toronto, Ontario

INDIA PALE ALE

1900

In 1878, Robert Davies left his brother, with whom he had operated the Don Brewery since 1871, to found the Dominion Brewery and build a new plant on Queen Street East. In 1893 he sold a controlling interest to a British syndicate, but remained as manager until 1899. One of Toronto's wealthiest people at the time, Davies also built the Don Valley Brickworks and owned a large number of Toronto taverns.

The brewery was acquired by E.P. Taylor's Canada Brewing Corporation in 1931, and closed in 1936 when Cosgrave's Dominion was formed. The building still stands, and the Dominion Pub—long a host of Toronto breweriana and buy/sell trade shows—is still popular today.

THE MONTREAL BREWING COMPANY
Montreal, Quebec

CUSHING'S PILSENER LAGER

Early 1900s

The Montreal Brewing Company can be traced back to 1840. Thomas Cushing became the manager in 1878 and subsequently the president. In 1909 it was absorbed by National Breweries and closed in 1910. The slogan "The Beer That Makes Milwaukee Jealous" was seen on the labels of various breweries in Canada.

"THE BEER THAT MAKES MILWAUKEE JEALOUS."

Cushing's

PILSENER LAGER

Brewed By
THE MONTREAL BREWING CO.
WITH PURE ARTESIAN WELL WATER.

ROCK SPRING BREWERY
Quebec City, Quebec

FOX HEAD BRAND
XX PORTER

Early 1900s

Established in 1895 by J.P. Côté and George E. Amyot, Rock Spring Brewery—as it was named in 1901—was located against a cliff where spring water was drawn for their beers.

Located in Quebec City, the brewery was in a relatively rural setting. Capitalizing on this, Côté and Amyot sought to distinguish themselves from competing breweries in the area, hence the fox head on the label. The fox motif became so recognizable that Rock Spring Brewery changed its name to Fox Head Brewery in 1910. The brewery became part of National Breweries and closed in 1916.

THE EATON BROTHERS BREWING COMPANY
Owen Sound, Ontario

XXX PORTER

1900

Originally founded in 1851 by Hamlin & Riddell Brewers, the Eaton Brothers Brewing Company was acquired by Christopher Eaton (no relation to the Toronto Eatons of department store fame) in 1883. It closed in 1906—earlier than most other Ontario breweries—when Owen Sound voters opted for Prohibition. Owen Sound was one of the first areas to go dry in Ontario, which put it out of business.

Dating between 1895 and 1906, this label features the goat's head usually seen in association with bock beer.

THE EATON BRO'S BREWING CO. LIMITED

OF OWEN SOUND.

XXX

TRADE MARK

PORTER

ORILLIA BREWING COMPANY
Orillia, Ontario

XXX PORTER

1900

The Orillia Brewing Company was established in 1882, but only operated under this name from 1895 to 1904, under J.A.P. Clarke, who was then the sole proprietor. It finally closed permanently when Prohibition started in 1915. This is a simple label for the time, but despite its understated appearance—or perhaps *because* of it—the design is strong, bold, and elegant.

THE ORILLIA BREWING CO.

XXX
PORTER

BOTTLED & DRAUGHT.

UNION BREWING LIMITED
Montreal, Quebec

IMPERIAL ALE

Circa 1900

This brewery dates back to 1891, with the name Union Brewing Company Limited adopted in 1896. It was taken over by National Breweries in 1909 and closed in 1920. This label dates from the turn of the twentieth century, circa 1900.

BRANDON BREWING COMPANY
Brandon, Manitoba

BRANDON LAGER

Early 1900s

In 1903, the Brandon Brewing Company started brewing ale, porter, and lager, only to have the brewery destroyed by fire in December of 1905. A new masonry brewery was built in 1906 and operated until 1919, when it was closed because of Prohibition. The illustration of the beaver on the label represents Canada's history with the Assiniboine River fur trade. The cluster of hop leaves, of course, is a nod to the ingredient used in beer.

DOMINION TEMPERANCE BREWERY
Montreal, Quebec

DOMO PORTER

Early 1900s

This short-lived brewery was first known as the Bassara Brewery and made temperance, stout, and porter-style beers between 1909 and 1910. Later, the Dominion Temperance Brewery operated, but for only three years, until 1916. At that time, Dominion became the Independent Brewery, which opened for only one year, closing as "normal" beers returned to Quebec: low-alcohol beer was unpopular—consumers either quit drinking or went to bootleggers. Because of all these different factors, Domo Porter's emphasis on temperance is intriguing, and it is one of the few labels that flaunts low alcohol content.

ELK VALLEY BREWING COMPANY
Michel, British Columbia

EXTRA FINE BREW

Early 1900s

Operating between 1908 to 1918, this brewery is likely the same plant that names Natal as its location (see page 58), as the two communities are close in proximity; in fact, Michel and Natal often redefined their borders. Michel was a mining town that had different locations due to mine expansion, and the brewery had a strong local market as the miners enjoyed beer after a strenuous shift. Indeed, the demand for beer drew a number of breweries to the area. Early British Columbia labels like this one are often specific to their regions.

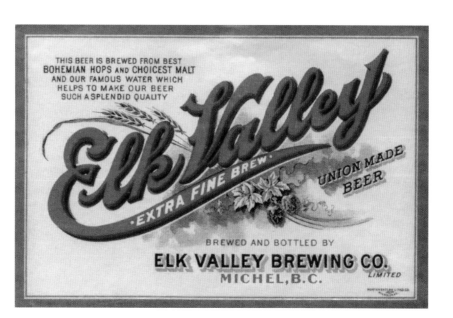

GOLDEN LION BREWING COMPANY
Prince Albert, Saskatchewan

PRINCE ALBERT BEER

Early 1900s

Originally established in 1896 as the Witteman Brewery, the Golden Lion Brewing Company took on its regal new name in 1904, and was known as such until the company closed in 1918.

This label dates from the early 1900s. Bordered by ornate scrolls, and bearing majestic imagery that aptly reflects the company's name, the label is die-cut, which was exceptional for label design of this era.

PRINCE ALBERT BEER

GOLDEN LION BREWING CO. LTD.

PRINCE ALBERT, SASK.

GOLDEN LION BREWING COMPANY
Prince Albert, Saskatchewan

XX PORTER

Early 1900s

On this label, which is more simple than the die-cut label for
Golden Lion's Prince Albert Beer (see page 45), we see the
majestic golden lion motif—though more diminutive in this
design than in Prince Albert's—with the lion flanked by two
x's. "XX" was used to indicate the strength of the beer; XXX
represents a beer of greater strength.

GOLDEN WEST BREWING COMPANY
Calgary, Alberta

GOLDEN WEST BEER

Early 1900s

This aptly designed label, which portrays the name of its company, was produced by the Golden West Brewing Company. In operation for twelve years (from 1906 to 1918), it closed after Prohibition was introduced in Alberta in 1916.

REGINA BREWING COMPANY
Regina, Saskatchewan

REGINA BEER
ROYAL BAVARIAN

Early 1900s

Founded in 1894, the Regina Brewing Company used this name from 1907 to 1915, when Prohibition forced it to close. The castle on the left-hand side of the label is a nod to the regal derivation of the name Regina, and the artwork beautifully represents an idyllic prairie landscape and sunset—as does the background for the Royal Bavarian label, which features the iconic German stein and Bavarian Monk.

SLEEMAN'S SPARKLING ALE

Early 1900s

In 1834, brewer John H. Sleeman arrived in Canada. He originally settled in St. David's, Ontario, and moved to Guelph in the 1840s, because the water there was similar to the water in Cornwall, England. In 1851, he opened the Silver Creek Brewery. His son, George Sleeman, eventually took over the business and led it to great success. Unfortunately, it was forced to shut down in 1933 when workers were caught smuggling beer over the border for delivery to Al Capone.

Five generations later, in the 1980s, John W. Sleeman received a book of family recipes, and he decided to resurrect the Sleeman family brewing legacy. It's difficult to accurately date this label, but it could be from the early 1900s. Note the interesting neck label, which shows that the beer was bottled expressly for J.S. Henderson, a grocery merchant in Kingston, Ontario.

ST. LAWRENCE BREWERY LIMITED
Cornwall, Ontario

SELECT PURE TABLE BEER

Early 1900s

The St. Lawrence Brewery Limited was first organized as the Cornwall Brewing Company in 1908 by a group from Sherbrooke, Quebec, who hoped to supply the nearby Quebec market. A new brick brewery was built beside the canal, and in 1909 it was incorporated as the St. Lawrence Brewery Limited.

The brands produced in this new brewery included this Select Brand Pure Table Beer, Cornwall Ale, Lager, and Porter. Production, however, came to a halt with the outbreak of WWI, which forced the brewery to switch to a "light" beer. The area voted dry in 1919, and the brewery closed in 1920.

PHOENIX BREWING COMPANY LIMITED
Phoenix, British Columbia

GENUINE EXTRA STOUT

1910

This brewery operated in Phoenix, British Columbia, from 1899 to 1920, first by brothers Julius and Andrew Mueller, and then under the name Phoenix Brewing Company from 1907 to 1920. Theodore Biner & Sons operated this brewery from 1905 to 1920. Note the fine print on this label promoting the quality of the beer.

ELK VALLEY BREWING
Natal, British Columbia

TEMPERANCE BEER

1910–1918

The Prohibition era in British Columbia ran from 1917 to 1921, and in compliance with Prohibition's restrictions, Elk Valley Brewing produced this "non-intoxicating liquor." One can only speculate how the hardworking miners in the local market received *this* version of beer. Also worth pondering: Did bootlegging take place in the area during that time? If so, the label's proclamation that the bottles were sterilized, and that the beer was bottled only at the Elk Valley brewery, could indicate that the poor sanitary practices of illegal brewers had caused undesirable results.

NON-INTOXICATING LIQUOR

TEMPERANCE

BOTTLED ONLY
AT THE BREWERY.
EVERY BOTTLE
STERILIZED

WINNING
THE WORLD
WITH
ELK QUALITY

BREW

WE GUARANTEE
THIS BEER TO BE BREWED FROM CHOICEST MATERIALS.

ELK VALLEY BREWING CO. LTD.

NATAL, B.C.

J.M. SPENARD

Trois Rivières, Quebec

J.M.S. PORTER

1912

This label design is true to the three rivers that inspired the artwork. J.M. Spenard was a short-lived brewery in Trois Rivières, from 1912 to 1919, with J.M. Spenard as manager from 1912 to 1916 and president from 1916 to 1919. The name was changed to La Brasserie des Trois Rivières in 1919, but the brewery eventually closed in 1923.

STRICTLY PURE J·M·S PORTER — J.M. SPENARD THREE RIVERS P.Q.

THE MEDICINE HAT BREWING COMPANY LIMITED
Medicine Hat, Alberta

HAT'S PORTER

1913–1920

From 1913 to 1920, this Prohibition-era non-intoxicating beer was produced by the Medicine Hat Brewing Company Limited. This delightfully creative label proclaims that the beer is non-intoxicating, yet "brewed from choice malt and best hops." The imagery of the top hat speaks to the name of the town, and the illustration of the early oil well is an interesting feature in that it's not directly related to the brewing industry. Perhaps the workers in those early days of Canada's petroleum industry enjoyed a refreshing bottle of this non-intoxicating porter at the end of a long, hard day.

ALEXANDER KEITH & SON LIMITED
Halifax, Nova Scotia

INDIA PALE ALE

1920s

Alexander Keith started brewing beer in Halifax in the 1820s, but the name Alexander Keith & Son Limited was not used until 1927. It continued under that name until 1972 when the Oland family, who had purchased the brewery in 1928, closed it and moved production to the Oland plant. Keith's IPA is still produced by Labatt's. The original brewery is now a brewpub and popular tourist attraction.

BRITISH AMERICAN BREWING COMPANY
Windsor, Ontario

BRITISH ALE

Mid-1920s

Early brewers who came to North America were mostly British, and brought with them ales, porters, and stouts. The British American Brewing Company was established in 1885 and survived Prohibition by making various 2.5% beers for the local market, and "stronger" beer for the export market. In 1925, Ontario laws were changed when Fergie's 4.4% Foam—named after Premier Howard Ferguson—was legalized, dating this colourful label, which showcases the factory, somewhere between 1924 and 1927. Note that the size of the brewery was sometimes exaggerated in such illustrations to make it seem bigger and more impressive.

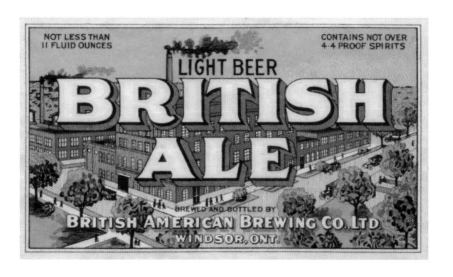

BRITISH AMERICAN BREWING COMPANY
Windsor, Ontario

CINCINNATI CREAM LAGER

1920s

In 1912, this famous Canadian beer was launched with a plain rectangular label. In 1927, after Prohibition ended in Ontario, the company created a new label and included this image of the "Handsome Waiter," which appeared on labels and on beer trays. Intricate, multicoloured labels such as this one were often created to prevent forgers from illegally reproducing labels for American versions of this brand. In 1985, "Cinci," as it was known in its final years, was re-launched by Molson in British Columbia, with a retro-style label that brought the handsome waiter to life once again for a short period.

THE CAPITAL BREWING COMPANY
Ottawa, Ontario

CAPITAL CREAM ALE

1920s

In 1899, the Capital Brewing Company was incorporated by Henry Kuntz of the extended Kuntz brewing family. Henry was born in Germany, but learned brewing in the United States before coming to Ottawa in 1899.

Early labels featured the original parliament building before it burned down in 1916; the new parliament building appeared on the label after it was rebuilt. The brewing company's only local competition was Bradings; both breweries survived Prohibition because of the nearby Quebec market. E.P. Taylor of Canadian Breweries Limited, who started in his family Bradings' Brewery, purchased the Capital Brewing Company in 1944 and merged the two as Bradings' Capital. However, all Capital brands were eliminated by 1945.

CREAM ALE

CAPITAL ALE

OTTAWA
ONT.

THE CAPITAL BREWING CO. LIMITED

LA BRASSERIE CHAMPLAIN LIMITÉE
Quebec City, Quebec

PORTER

1920s

La Brasserie Champlain Limitée was established in 1911 in Quebec City, acquired by National Breweries in 1948, and closed in 1952. The design for the Champlain beer labels, registered in 1916, featured the famous statue of Samuel de Champlain in Quebec City, and was used in numerous Champlain beers, including this porter.

Champlain labels in the 1920s were typically two colours; later, a four-colour label for Champlain Select Ale was used, featuring an artist's illustration of Champlain's head and shoulders.

CRONMILLER & WHITE BREWING COMPANY LIMITED
Welland, Ontario

INDIAN HEAD ALL MALT ALE

1920s

Originally established in my hometown of Port Colborne in 1857 by Jacob North, this brewery was taken over and run by Henry Cronmiller and Thomas White until Prohibition closed it in 1919. The dormant company was acquired by the Iroquois Brewing Company at Buffalo, New York, and reopened in nearby Welland in 1925, producing 4.4% beer for the local market. Many of the labels featured the Iroquois logo. I had the pleasure of interviewing Mrs. Thom White in 1976 when she was 100 years of age, and enjoyed hearing the story of her upbringing in the original brewery in the 1880s.

DAWES BREWERIES
Lachine, Quebec

BLACK HORSE ALE

1920s

The Dawes brewery dates back to 1811, when Thomas Dawes established it in Lachine. It ran there until 1926, when operations were consolidated in the former Imperial Brewery on St. Maurice Street in Montreal. Dawes was dropped from the brewery name in favour of the Dow Brewery in 1952 (see page 120). The horse, as seen on the label, was featured on a number of other promotional items, such as beer trays, small statues in various materials, postcards, and other forms of advertising. This design is a very early version; the horse motif became more refined in later years.

FERNIE-FORT STEELE BREWING COMPANY
Fernie, British Columbia

LION BRAND PORTER

1920s

In 1909, the Fernie-Fort Steele Brewing Company opened in a new masonry plant, a year after its wood structure brewery was destroyed in the Great Fernie Fire of 1908. It operated under this name until 1934, when it became the Fernie Brewing Company. With Prohibition taking place between 1917 and 1921 in British Columbia, the Fernie-Fort Steele Brewing Company created this unique, original, non-intoxicating porter, with "wholesome and invigorating" as its selling point.

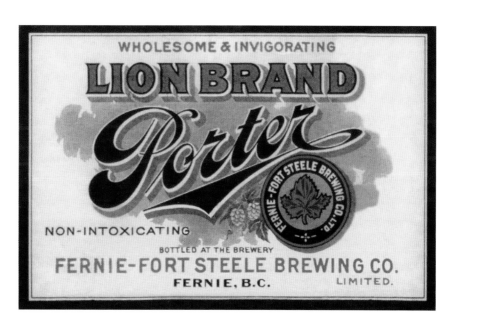

THE KUNTZ BREWERY LIMITED
Waterloo, Ontario

KUNTZ HALF & HALF
KUNTZ LAGERINE

Early 1920s

The Kuntz Brewery, which dates back to 1840 when David Kuntz founded the Spring Brewery, survived Prohibition by brewing light beers such as Half & Half and Lagerine. These guaranteed 2.5% proof spirits or less, and predated 1924 when 4.4% beers were legalized. The company also produced soft drinks during the 1920s and 1930s.

NEWFOUNDLAND BREWING COMPANY LIMITED
St. John's, Newfoundland

AMBRALE

1920s

In 1893 the Newfoundland Brewing Company Limited was established, and in 1918, the name was changed to Newfoundland Brewing Limited. Prohibition in this province lasted from 1917 to 1924 when this low-alcohol beer—less than 2%—would have been sold. The brewery is still operated by Molson, which acquired it in 1962.

SILVER SPRING BREWERY LIMITED
Victoria, British Columbia

SILVER FOAM

Circa 1920

This was a non-intoxicating beer produced before Prohibition in BC (1917–1921). Silver Spring Brewery Limited operated from 1903 to 1909 in one location in Victoria, then moved to a new location where it was open from 1909 to 1957.

TERRIS BEVERAGE COMPANY
Saint John, New Brunswick

WHITE STAR HOP BEER

1920s

This temperance "beer" was produced in Saint John, New Brunswick, by the short-lived Terris Beverage Company, which operated from 1915 to 1927. The dramatic design of the label was guaranteed to attract attention to the brew.

NORTHWEST BREWING COMPANY LIMITED
Edmonton, Alberta

BOHEMIAN MAID BEER

1924

The Northwest Brewing Company traces its roots back to 1896. It closed for eight years—between 1916 and 1924—during Prohibition, but reopened and operated as a new brewing company until 1958, when the Calgary Brewing and Malting Company bought control. Subsequently, it changed the brewery name to Bohemian Maid Brewing, featuring its iconic beer. Note the use of the term "cereal brew" and the lack of indication of alcohol percentage. In 1958, the Bohemian Brewing Company—a later iteration of the Northwest Brewing Company—released Bohemian Maid Beer with an updated label.

REGAL BREWING COMPANY LIMITED
Hamilton, Ontario

GOLD SPUR ALE

Mid-1920s

This brewery was originally founded in 1873 by David Kuntz of the extended Kuntz family, and called it the Dominion Brewery. It survived Prohibition, and in 1936 was merged with the Taylor & Bate Brewery in St. Catharines, which was then closed. The Regal Brewery in Hamilton took on the Taylor & Bate name for two years before it too was closed in 1938. After Prohibition, they issued a beer tray featuring the rooster seen on the Gold Spur Ale label. The word "spur" in the beer's rather unusual name refers to the spike on the back of a rooster's leg.

TAYLOR & BATE LIMITED
St. Catharines, Ontario

NIAGARA SPRAY

Mid-1920s

Taylor & Bate was originally established in St. Catharines by James Taylor in 1874. Thomas B. Bate joined the company in 1857, which meant a company name change to Taylor & Bate. It was acquired by the Brewing Corporation of Ontario in 1930 and closed in 1936 when it merged with the Regal Brewery in Hamilton, where it operated for two years. The Taylor & Bate brewery name was revived in Stratford in 1988 and eventually ended up back in St. Catharines in 1998.

This iconic Niagara Spray beer dates from the 1920s and was brought back to life by the modern brewery in St. Catharines—though the brewery closed in 2001.

THE SASKATOON BREWING COMPANY LIMITED
Saskatoon, Saskatchewan

LIQUID BREAD

1926

Established in 1905 as the Hoeschen-Wentzler Brewing Company Limited, the company was eventually renamed the Saskatoon Brewing Company Limited in 1915, as many Canadian breweries dropped German names during WWI. Liquid Bread was introduced in 1926 with an ad that boasted, "One of America's most successful brewmasters is in charge of the making of 'Liquid Bread'—not the same beer with a new badge," letting customers know that this was a distinctly new beer made with a new recipe.

EMPIRE BREWING COMPANY
Brandon, Manitoba

EMPIRE LAGER

Late 1920s

The Empire Brewing Company built a new masonry brewery in 1903 after a disastrous fire destroyed the original plant. The company was acquired by the Canadian Brewing Corporation in 1928, which merged with the Brewing Corporation of Ontario. The brewery closed in 1931; this label dates from the late 1920s. Note how the label features a map with the areas of the British Empire highlighted in red.

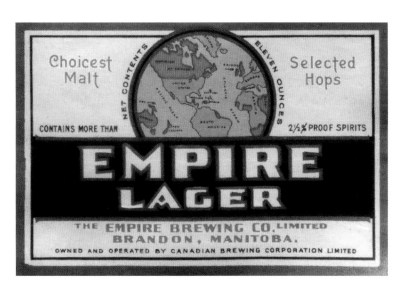

EMPIRE DRY PALE GINGER ALE

1928

Many breweries in Canada also produced soft drinks, as it proved to be the only way to get the brewery's name known to the public during a time when Canada's alcohol advertising laws were archaic and restrictive. Selling soft drinks also kept plants in operation during Prohibition.

Empire operated in Brandon from 1903 to 1931 (see page 96). There were other brewing companies that also produced soft drinks, including Calgary Brewing and Malting in Alberta, and, in Ontario, Kuntz and O'Keefe.

A
PALE DRY
GINGER ALE

PREFERRED
FOR ITS
EXCELLENCE

CONTENTS 6½ FLUID OUNCES

EMPIRE DRY

PALE GINGER ALE

THE EMPIRE BREWING CO. LIMITED
BRANDON, MANITOBA
OWNED AND OPERATED BY
CANADIAN BREWING CORPORATION
LIMITED

FRONTENAC BREWERIES
Montreal, Quebec

INDIA PALE EXPORT ALE

Late 1920s

Brasserie Frontenac was incorporated in 1911 and opened late in 1913. This label dates from the late 1920s, and on bottles shipped to the United States, it was stamped with the word "export." On beer trays, envelopes, and letterhead, Frontenac Breweries used a picture of its facilities. In 1927, it was taken over by National Breweries, only to be sold to Canadian Breweries Limited in 1951. Brewing ended here in April 1961, and the plant was subsequently demolished.

BIÈRE **FRONTENAC** ALE

BREWED IN CANADA TO COMPLY WITH
THE REGULATIONS OF THE UNITED STATES

EXPORT

BREWED IN CANADA TO COMPLY WITH
THE REGULATIONS OF THE UNITED STATES
CONTENTS 11 FLUID OUNCES

FRONTENAC

EXPORT ALE

FRONTENAC BREWERIES
LIMITED
MONTREAL

THIS LABEL REGISTERED

DOES NOT CONTAIN MORE THAN 4 PER CENTUM OF ALCOHOL BY VOLUME

MACPHERSON BREWING COMPANY LIMITED
Winnipeg, Manitoba

OLD SQUIRE ALE

Late 1920s

MacPherson Brewing Company Limited operated under this name for a very short period (1926–1930) with H.C. MacPherson as president. From 1930 to 1963 it was known as the Fort Garry Brewery Limited and was acquired by Molson in 1960. The colourful label for Old Squire Ale dates from the late 1920s.

VANCOUVER BREWERIES LIMITED
Vancouver, British Columbia

DUTCH GIRL LAGER

Late 1920s

Vancouver Breweries Limited was established in 1918 and operated under this name until 1957, finally closing in 1990 when Molson and Carling-O'Keefe merged. This is a distinct and original brand and label for that time, and unusual in that it featured a Dutch theme.

DUTCH GIRL LAGER

BEER

NET CONTENTS
12 FLUID
OUNCES

CONTAINS
OVER 8%
PROOF SPIRITS

BREWED AND BOTTLED BY
VANCOUVER BREWERIES LTD
VANCOUVER, B.C. CANADA

NEW EDMONTON BREWERIES LIMITED
Edmonton, Alberta

YELLOWHEAD BEER

1927–1933

This is a gorgeous, creative, and complex label for this brand, which advertised its product as "Brewed as a Beer Should Be" from "Pure Mountain Water" and "Western Canadian Barley" during the late 1920s and early 1930s. The label's artwork suggests progress, with the group of travellers on horses on one side of the Yellowhead Mountain—which sits on the Alberta/ BC border—and the train on the other.

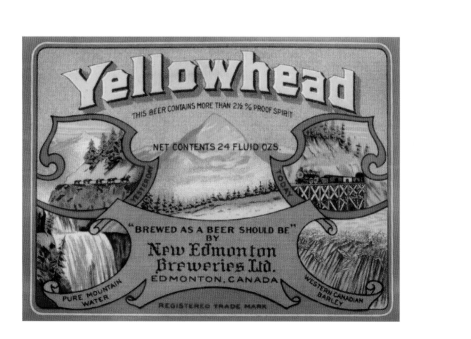

BAVARIAN BREWING COMPANY
St. John's, Newfoundland

THREE STAR LAGER

1930s

Three Star Lager was an early low-alcohol beer from the Bavarian Brewing Company—where Blue Star became the main brand—and it remains a local favourite of Newfoundlanders to this very day. Bavarian was purchased by Labatt in 1962, and the brewery is still in operation.

Three Star ★★★

Lager

Contents 12 Fluid Ounces

Made by
**Bavarian
Brewing** Ltd.
St. John's
Nfld

GOVT. LICENSE NO. 33
EXCISE DUTY PAID BY BOTTLER

BIXEL BREWING AND MALTING COMPANY
Brantford, Ontario

BIXEL'S FAMOUS LAGER BEER

1930s

Originally established in Strathroy, Ontario, in 1859, Bixel Brewing and Malting Company was relocated to Brantford, Ontario, in 1888 by the Bixel brothers: Cyrus, Oscar, and Arthur. After Prohibition in 1927, the brewery resumed the production of beer, and operated as a family-owned business until it was sold to Canadian Breweries in 1944 and closed. In 1990, a new Bixel Brewing and Malting Company revived production of Bixel beer, with an updated version of the 1930s label on a stubby bottle, but production lasted only for a year.

CARLING BREWERIES LIMITED
London, Ontario

BLACK AND WHITE
SPECIAL BREWED BEER

Early 1930s

The Carling name dates back to 1840 when Thomas Carling started brewing beer in London, Ontario. In 1930, Carling was acquired by the Brewing Corporation of Canada. The plant closed in 1936 when Carling was merged with the Kuntz Brewery in Waterloo as Carling-Kuntz. This vivid label, and its neckband with the charming Boston terrier, dates from the early 1930s. The label mentions London and Montreal, but Carling beers were only bottled in Montreal at that time.

COSGRAVE EXPORT BREWERY COMPANY
Toronto, Ontario

COSGRAVE'S CANADA'S BEST LAGER BEER

1930

This brewery dates back to at least 1844, but Patrick Cosgrave did not become involved until 1863. Several name changes followed: in 1866 it was known as the West Toronto Brewery; then, in 1872, it went by the name Cosgrave and Company. The name Cosgrave Export Brewery was adopted in 1930 and used until 1936 when it was merged with the Dominion Brewery. At that time, it became known as Cosgrave's Dominion Brewery. On this label, we see a rendition of a formidable brewery, but, as mentioned earlier, this was often an artistic embellishment designed to impress consumers.

COSGRAVE EXPORT BREWERY COMPANY
Toronto, Ontario

OLD MUNICH LAGER BEER

Early 1930s

Controlled and operated by the Brewing Corporation of
Canada, this label dates back to the early 1930s. The whimsical
artwork depicts eleven elves at varying stages of the brewing
process. It shows them working with fire, which suggests that
the beer was "fire brewed"—a method that differed from those
that used boilers and steam. Cosgrave's Old Munich Lager
Beer disappeared around the beginning of WWII, possibly
because of its German name.

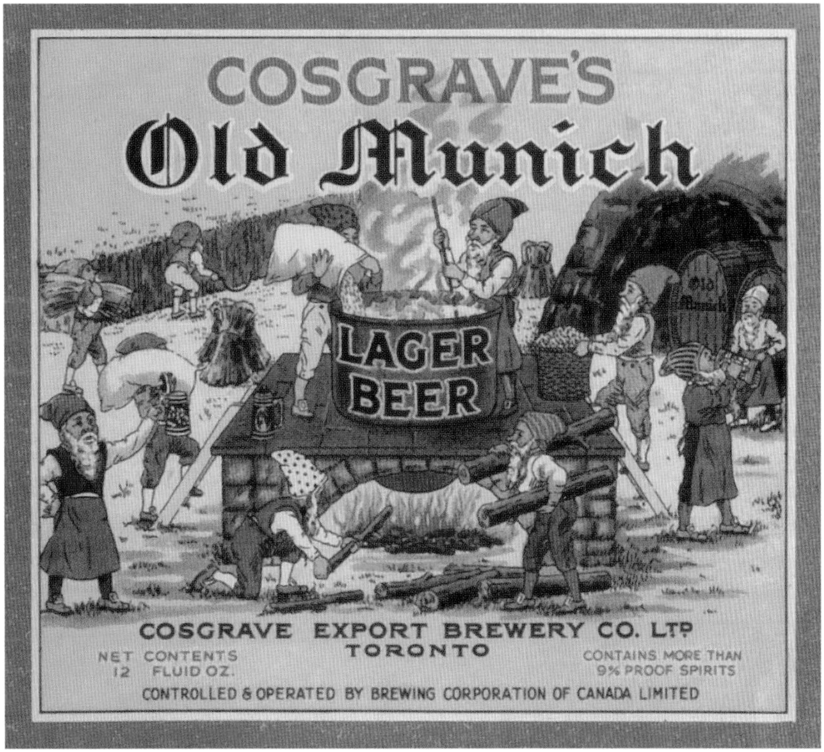
COSGRAVE'S
Old Munich
LAGER BEER
Old Munich
COSGRAVE EXPORT BREWERY CO. LTD
TORONTO
NET CONTENTS
12 FLUID OZ.
CONTAINS MORE THAN
9% PROOF SPIRITS
CONTROLLED & OPERATED BY BREWING CORPORATION OF CANADA LIMITED

DOMINION BREWERY COMPANY
Toronto, Ontario

WHITE SEAL BEER

1930s

White Seal Beer was a Manitoba brand—hailing from Dominion Brewery's sister brewery, Kiewel Brewing—created for the Ontario market from 1931 to 1936. It was one of the first brands to traverse provincial borders. Unusual for the era is the assurance on the label that the product is free of chemicals and preservatives. The eye-catching diamond logo was used for several different Kiewel beers.

DOW BREWERY LIMITED
Montreal, Quebec

DOW ALE

1930s

The Dow labels evolved slowly over the late 1800s and into the 1900s. This version was used in the 1930s. The Dow Brewery name was discontinued in Quebec by Canadian Breweries in favour of the O'Keefe name and brand in 1967.

JOHN H. MOLSON & BROTHERS
Montreal, Quebec

MOLSON'S EXPORT ALE

1930s

This is a 1930s version of the label for Molson Export Ale, a brand that dates back to the early 1900s, used by a brewery that dates back to 1786. The label features a design that changed very little for many years. The anchor motif may be a nod to John H. Molson's involvement in the steamship industry. In 2003, Molson honoured the 100th anniversary of the brand with a heritage edition of labels from 1903, 1933 (shown on opposite page), 1955, 1957, and 1962.

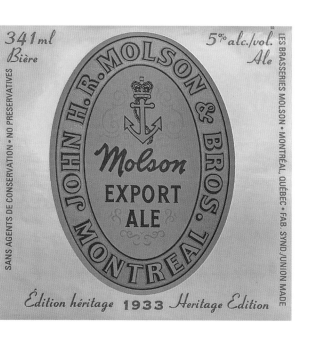

TAYLOR & BATE LIMITED
St. Catharines, Ontario

SILVER SPIRE ALE

Early 1930s

Silver Spire Ale was one of a series of beers released by Taylor & Bate Limited after the company established the radio station CKTB in St. Catharines, hence the radio tower that features prominently in the label's design. The brewery's ownership of the radio station did not last long, however, as the Ontario government forced Taylor & Bate to sell it due to strict regulations around where and how alcohol was advertised. Taylor & Bate did, however, continue to use Silver Spire as a brand name, which appeared on beer trays and tip trays. The radio station is still on the air to this day, under the same call letters.

RED BALL BREWERY LIMITED
Saint John, New Brunswick

OLD TAVERN INDIA PALE ALE

1930s

Red Ball Brewery Limited dates back to 1833. The name Red Ball was used as early as 1903, but this label would date from the post-1930 use of the name—after the brewery had been purchased by George W.C. Oland, whose Halifax brewery had been destroyed in the 1917 Halifax explosion.

Old Tavern
SPARKLING OLD ALE · VIELLE BIERE MOUSSEUSE
PALE ALE

BREWED AND BOTTLED BY RED BALL BREWERY LTD., SAINT JOHN, N.B., CANADA

Old Tavern

SINCE 1833

BREWED FROM
PURE MALT
AND HOPS

INDIA ALE PALE

CONTENTS 22 FLUID OZS. BRITISH

ROCK BREWERY LIMITED
Preston, Ontario

ROCK SPRINGS LAGER BEER

1930

This brewery, located in Preston near a natural spring, was established by George and Henry Bernhardt as the Rock (Springs) Brewery in 1846. The Bernhardt family remained in control until 1917, when it was closed until Prohibition ended in 1927. This label dates from circa 1930, before the brewery permanently closed in 1933.

DREWRYS REGINA LIMITED
Regina, Saskatchewan

MUNICH STYLE BEER

1935–1936

This brewery operated under the name Drewrys Regina Limited from 1935 to 1953, but was originally founded as the Adanac Brewery Company in 1928. In 1935, Western Breweries Limited, a holding company, acquired Adanac, and in 1935 changed the name to Drewrys Regina Limited.

This label was only in use from 1935 to 1936; references to Germany were removed from most Canadian beer labels when the war began, because of anti-German sentiment. The label design for Munich Style Beer features a German drinking scene similar to its sister brand, Salvator Beer (see page 154).

HUETHER BREWING COMPANY LIMITED
Kitchener, Ontario

BLUE TOP BEER

Mid-1930s

The C.N. Huether Berlin Lion Brewery dates back to 1900. In 1919, the city of Berlin, Ontario, changed its name to Kitchener due to the widespread anti-German sentiment that came with the war. Presumably for the same reason, the brewery was renamed the Huether Brewery Limited.

The Blue Top brand name was adopted in the early 1930s, and subsequently the company became Blue Top Brewing Company Limited. Its promotional material included colourful Blue Top key rings, blue tops, ashtrays, and beer tray mats to showcase its various brands of Blue Top beers.

NET CONTENTS
12 FLUID OUNCES

CONTAINS 9%
PROOF SPIRITS

BLUE TOP

100% PURE
MALT & HOPS

GUARANTEED
WELL AGED

BEER

HUETHER BREWING COMPANY LIMITED
KITCHENER ONTARIO

REGISTERED

STAR BREWING COMPANY LIMITED
North Battleford, Saskatchewan

WENTZLER'S STAR BOCK

Mid-1930s

The Star Brewing Company Limited was established in 1927 and operated until 1937. It was owned by Fred Wentzler from 1929 until his death in 1934. As with many bock labels, this one features the image of a goat, said to be the German symbol for bock beer, which originated in Einbeck. The German word for "billy goat" is *ziegenbock*, a word similar to the name Einbeck, which is probably why a bearded goat is seen in the artwork of many of these labels.

TAYLOR & BATE LIMITED
Hamilton, Ontario

REGAL BEER

1936–1937

Although Regal Beer dates back to the early 1900s and was still being brewed in the same location when this label was produced, the brewery's name had changed. E.P. Taylor and his Canadian Breweries Limited closed the Taylor & Bate Brewery in St. Catharines in 1936 and merged it with the Regal Brewery in Hamilton. This merger was short-lived, and the brewery was closed in 1938.

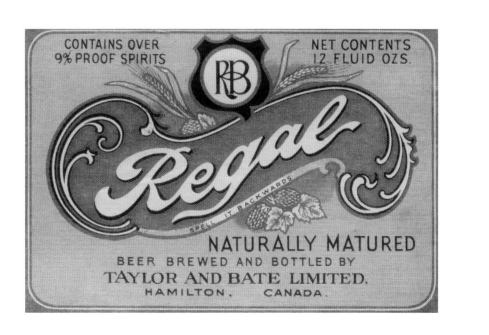

WALKERVILLE BREWERY LIMITED
Walkerville, Ontario

ROB ROY ALE

1930s

The Walkerville Brewery Limited was founded in 1890, by Hiram Walker of distillery fame. It was first called the Walkerville Brewing & Malting Company, and was renamed the Walkerville Brewery Limited in 1899. It was known by this name until 1944 when it was acquired by Canadian Breweries Limited. Rob Roy Ale was introduced before 1910, but its vivid label dates from the 1930s. The brewery was closed in 1956, but in 1998, a new craft brewery resumed production of beer in an empty Hiram Walker warehouse under the Walkerville Brewery name.

ACE HIGH BREWERY LIMITED
Guelph, Ontario

BURTON STYLE ALE

1938–1939

In 1933, Sleeman's ceased operations in Guelph after its license was revoked for bootlegging. Jockey Club Brewery Limited was founded after Sleeman's closure. It became its short-lived successor, and was subsequently reorganized as Ace High Brewery in 1938. Operations ceased in 1939 after just one year, when the brewery produced Ace High Burton Style Ale. The label—the only one we know of—was inspired by the ace playing card. Pat Quinn, the manager, also had his signature on the label, which is an unusual design detail.

CONTAINS OVER 9% PROOF SPIRITS NET CONTENTS 12 FLUID OZS.

AGED IN OAK

A BURTON STYLE

Ace ♥ High
ALE

WE GUARANTEE SPRING WATER USED TO
BREW THIS 100% PURE ALE

Pat Quinn
MGR.

ACE HIGH BREWERY LIMITED
GUELPH, ONT.

CAPILANO BREWING COMPANY LIMITED
Vancouver, British Columbia

ACE LAGER

Late 1930s

This simple but memorable label was used by the Capilano Brewing Company between 1936 and 1944, when the name of the brewery changed to Sicks' Capilano Brewery. The name change was adopted to promote the connection to Sicks' House of Lethbridge, the cornerstone of Sicks' chain of breweries.

Because this label was essentially black and white at a time when most labels were multicoloured, the design is striking and out of the ordinary. Molson purchased the brewery in 1959, and Molson products are still brewed at this same location today.

HOFER BREWING COMPANY LIMITED
LaSalle, Ontario

HOFER SELECT LAGER BEER

Late 1930s

This brewery was established in 1928 in the suburbs of Windsor, Ontario. Partners included Carl Hofer, who gave his name to the brewery and this colourful label for its Select Ale. J.K. Hofer was manager in 1935–1936. The brewery was acquired by Canadian Breweries Limited in 1939, and then closed. This label design is a subtle Canadian imitation—one of several—of the American Budweiser label.

We Guarantee that this Beverage is a full
weight Lager, Healthful, Refreshing, Nutritious
and fully Aged.

JKHofer

TRADE MARK

HOFER BREWING COMPANY

CONTENTS II
FLUID OZS.

CONTAINS 9%
PROOF SPIRIT

HOFER
Select Lager
BEER

THE HOFER BREWING COMPANY LTD., LA SALLE, ONTARIO.

OLD VIENNA BEER

1930s

This Toronto brewery dates back to the 1840s, when it was already known as the Victoria Brewery. When Eugene O'Keefe and a group of partners purchased the brewery in 1862, they retained the name as the brewery was situated on Victoria Street in Toronto. The brewery prospered, and Eugene O'Keefe became one of Toronto's biggest philanthropists. Old Vienna Beer dates back to the 1930s when this vibrant label was used. O.V., as the beer is now called, is still brewed by Molson. The whimsical scene, as illustrated on the early version of the label, gave way in later years to a more streamlined design.

KUNTZ BREWERY LIMITED/
CARLING-KUNTZ BREWERIES LIMITED
Waterloo, Ontario

OLD GERMAN LAGER
OLD TAVERN LAGER

1939

Old German Lager predates 1936 when the Carling plant in London, Ontario, was closed, merged with the Kuntz plant in Waterloo, and renamed Carling-Kuntz Breweries Limited. That name was used until 1940 when the Kuntz name was dropped entirely. In 1939, the brand name was changed from Old German Lager to Old Tavern Lager because of the anti-German sentiment that came with WWII. After making the necessary modifications, the brewery continued to picture this lighthearted German drinking scene on its label for a few years.

RED BALL BREWERY/OLAND'S BREWERY LIMITED
Saint John, New Brunswick

OLAND'S AGED DINNER ALE

1930s

Bearing both the Red Ball and Oland name and dating from the 1930s, this label illustrates the Reversing Falls—still one of the most popular tourist attractions in Saint John, New Brunswick. Whenever I visited the Moosehead Brewery in Saint John, I would make a special trip to the nearby Reversing Falls, simply to marvel at this natural wonder.

OLAND'S
AGED
BREWED FROM PURE MALT & HOPS
DINNER ALE

CONTENTS 11 FLUID OUNCES – THIS ALE CONTAINS MORE THAN 7% PROOF SPIRITS

OLAND'S
ESTABLISHED 1828

REVERSING
FALLS
SAINT JOHN, N.B.

BREWED FROM PURE MALT & HOPS

INDIA PALE

DINNER ALE

BREWED AT THE RED BALL BREWERY – OLANDS BREWERY LTD, SAINT JOHN, N.B. CANADA

THE BIG HORN BREWING COMPANY LIMITED
Calgary, Alberta

HORN BRAND BEER

1940s

A perfect example of how breweries are often acquired and renamed, this brewery was originally founded as the Mountain Spring Brewery in 1912, and rebranded as Silver Spray in 1915. Calgary Brewing & Malting Company purchased the company in 1927 and renamed it the Big Horn Brewing Company—the name by which it was known until 1961, when it was acquired by Canadian Breweries. As bighorn sheep were, and continue to be, indigenous to the mountainous areas of Alberta, it is quite fitting that the rugged, majestic creature adorns this label from the 1940s.

THE DREWRYS LIMITED
Winnipeg, Manitoba

SALVATOR BEER

1940s

Salvator is a strong, German-style beer with a centuries-old history, and was produced by several breweries in Canada, including Reinhardt's in Toronto. This label, from The Drewrys Limited in Winnipeg, Manitoba, dates from the 1940s. Its artwork captures the joviality of sharing this "old Bohemian brew" with friends, and proclaims that it hails from "an old Bohemian formula"—rather curious, considering the term "Bohemia" refers to a region in what is now known as the Czech Republic.

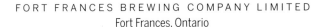

FORT FRANCES BREWING COMPANY LIMITED
Fort Frances, Ontario

49 CANADIAN LAGER

1940s

In 1925, the Fort Frances Brewing Company was established, and went on until 1964 when William Beck purchased it and changed its name to Beck Brewing Company. This beer was exported by Viger Beverages across the 49th parallel, as indicated on the label, into International Falls, Minnesota. Dating from the 1940s, this label caught my eye as it's a local brand, made exclusively for export to International Falls, Minnesota.

JOHN LABATT LIMITED
London, Ontario

EXPORT INDIA PALE ALE

1940s

This case label is an example of the breweries' contribution to restrictions placed on all aspects of industry in Canada during WWII. Customers were encouraged to return beer cases for reuse, and Canadian brewing companies collected funds to buy cigarettes to send to the troops overseas. Many of Labatt's labels did not change drastically for over seventy-five years, as shown by this design's similarity to the 1889 IPA label.

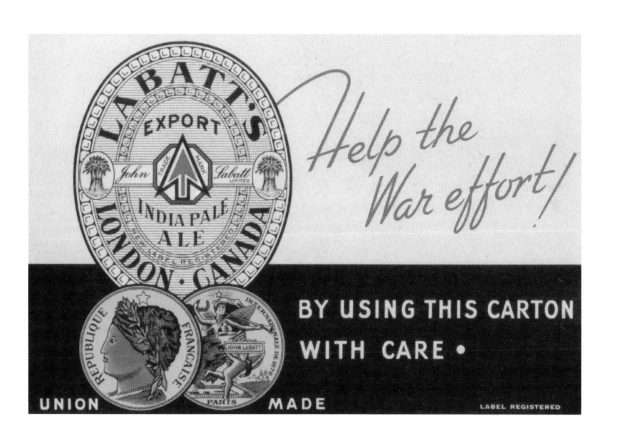

LAKE OF THE WOODS BREWING COMPANY
Kenora, Ontario

OLD STOCK ALE

1940s

This brewery was established in 1899, when Kenora was known as Rat Portage. The brewery had a troubled history contending with Prohibition, opening and closing for various periods during the early 1900s and during Prohibition. This company name and colourful label dates from the 1940s, and depicts the natural attributes of the area. The brewery also issued two beautiful and extremely rare porcelain beer trays dating from the 1930s.

THE RIEDLE BREWERY LIMITED
Winnipeg, Manitoba

BLACK TOP

1940s

Dating back to 1904, the brewery was known by the name
Riedle Brewery from 1923 to 1949, and as Grants from 1949
to 1957, when it was purchased by Canadian Breweries Limited.
Dating from the 1940s, the label features the image of a goat,
as seen on many bock beer labels.

SICKS' REGINA BREWERY LIMITED
Regina, Saskatchewan

OLD STYLE PILSNER BEER

1940s

Established in 1907, this brewery operated under the name
Regina Breweries until 1917 when it closed. Fritz Sick purchased
the brewery in 1924 and ran it under this name until 1944 when
he added his name to the company.

Here we see two versions of a label—one featuring an
older plane, train, and automobile, and the other as a more
modern version. This label also has the "6" logo, a play on
the name "Sicks." This brand is still sold by Molson, which
acquired Sicks' in 1958; the labels today feature depictions
of the earlier forms of transportation.

SHEA'S WINNIPEG BREWERY LIMITED
Winnipeg, Manitoba

SHEA'S SPECIAL XMAS ALE

1947

Dating from 1947, this seasonal ale was produced by Shea's Winnipeg Brewery Limited, which was known by that name from 1926 to 1958 with the Shea family in control. Labatt's purchased the company in 1958. I speculate that this Christmas label says "Xmas" because there wasn't enough space on this narrow oval label to spell out "Christmas."

THE SASKATOON BREWING COMPANY LIMITED
Saskatoon, Saskatchewan

'67 BEER

1947

The Saskatoon Brewing Company name was adopted in 1915; the original name was Hoeschen-Wentzler Brewing Company Limited (est. 1906). This vibrant label dates from 1947, the eightieth anniversary of Confederation, not 1967 as one might think from the name. This picture is quite similar to the famous one that shows the Fathers of Confederation meeting in Charlottetown in 1864 (not 1867). The Saskatchewan Liquor Commission forced the brewery to remove this label from the market. Why? Liquor control boards from province to province had their own regulations—much as they do now—so it's possible that the illustration on the label was too similar to the famous Robert Harris painting.

WESTERN CANADA BREWERIES LIMITED
Winnipeg, Manitoba

STANDARD LAGER

1940s

Western Canada Breweries was formed in 1927 to control the assets of several Western Canadian breweries, including Drewrys in Winnipeg. This label dates from the 1940s and is a close knock-off of the American Budweiser label, a design that was adopted by several breweries in Canada.

CRANBROOK BREWING COMPANY LIMITED
Cranbrook, British Columbia

BAVARIAN EXPORT

Late 1940s

Cranbrook Brewing Company opened in 1912, closed from 1919 to 1921 during Prohibition, and reopened in 1921. This label has a rather complex design for the time, and depicts what could have been a typical scene of the brewing process, which often took place in Bavarian monastery breweries in Germany as a way to create additional income for the church.

SICKS' REGINA BREWERY LIMITED
Regina, Saskatchewan

YE OLDE ENGLISH NUT BROWN ALE

1948–1958

The Regina Brewing Company was established in 1907 and operated until 1915, when it closed. Fritz Sick reopened the brewery on the same site in 1924 and renamed it Sicks' Regina Brewery Limited in 1944. It operated under this name until 1959, when Molson acquired all of the Sicks' breweries.

SICKS' EDMONTON BREWERY LIMITED
Edmonton, Alberta

REX PILSNER

1944–1959

Here we see two similar labels, equal in creativity and complexity. The earlier version of the label shows the car travelling along an Alberta mountain road; the later version incorporates many of the earlier design elements that depict the oil, grain, and mining industries so prominent in Alberta. The more recent version features Sicks' name, which indicates the company's name change in 1944 from Edmonton Breweries Limited to Sicks' Edmonton Brewery Limited.

CALGARY BREWING & MALTING COMPANY LIMITED
Calgary, Alberta

MOKINSTSIS

1950s

The Calgary Brewing & Malting Company was founded by
A.E. Cross in 1892 and was eventually acquired by Canadian
Breweries in 1961. The logo, with a buffalo head set inside the
curve of a horseshoe, was designed by A.E. Cross himself,
shortly after the company's inception. The name of the beer,
Mokinstsis, is the Blackfoot place name for Calgary, making
it one of the most interesting and extraordinary beer names
used in Canada.

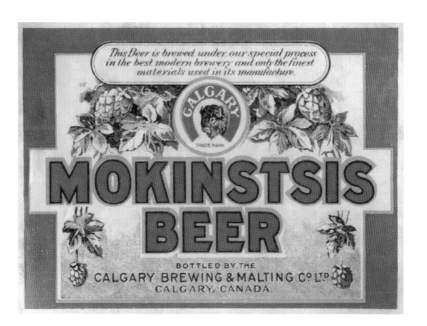

JOHN LABATT LIMITED
London, Ontario

50 ANNIVERSARY ALE

1950

50 Anniversary Ale, which eventually became known as Labatt's 50, was introduced in 1950 to commemorate fifty years of service to the brewery by brothers Hugh and John Labatt. The letter on the back of the label tells the full story about the beer and the Labatt family as the fourth generation enters the company.

ALL THE BODY AND CHARACTER TRADITIONAL WITH LABATTS

Anniversary Ale
50

A SMOOTHER LIGHTER FLAVOUR

L.C.B.O.

UNION MADE

Mr. John Labatt's

OWN SPECIALLY BREWED
GOLDEN

Anniversary Ale
50

BREW NO. 161   1950

JOHN LABATT LIMITED
LONDON
CANADA

LABEL REGISTERED

CONTENTS 12 FLUID OUNCES

Dear Friends:

Thank you for mak-
ing Anniversary Ale so
popular. It is a regular
Labatt brand now and will
always be brewed in accordance with my original recipe.

As a director and senior brewing
consultant, I continue to supervise
all Labatt's brewing. I shall
assist, also, in training my son, the
fourth John Labatt, who is now
working in the brewery.

Thanks, again, for your
confidence and support.

John T. Labatt

P.S.: I won the bet
with brother
Hugh.

MOOSEHEAD BREWERIES LIMITED
Fairville, New Brunswick

ALPINE LAGER BEER

1950s

Moosehead Breweries Limited, founded in 1867 by one branch of the Oland family, is Canada's oldest independent brewery. It is still located in Saint John, New Brunswick, and owned and operated by the sixth generation of the Olands.

Here we have a vibrant version of the Moosehead Alpine Lager Beer label dating from the fifties. The label proudly extols the virtues of this beer, proclaiming that it has been "brewed from an old European recipe." It was first developed and brewed by P.W. Oland in 1937.

Alpine
STAR OF EXCELLENCE   1ST PRIZE BRUSSELS 1950
LAGER BEER

NET CONTENTS 12 FLUID OZS. BRITISH
famous for its flavour
Alpine
LAGER BEER
TRADE MARK REG'D
BREWED FROM AN OLD EUROPEAN RECIPE - THIS BEER IS HEALTHFUL REFRESHING - NUTRITIOUS FULLY MATURED AND AGED
MOOSEHEAD BREWERIES LTD., FAIRVILLE, N.B. CANADA.

OLD COMRADES BREWERY LIMITED
Windsor, Ontario

OLD COMRADES BEER LAGER

1950

The first brewery on this site, Tecumseh Brewing Company Limited, operated from 1928 to 1929. It operated as the St. Clair Brewing Company Limited from 1929 to 1930, and evolved into the Tecumseh Brewery Company in 1931. Between 1932 and 1948, the building was used as a cannery.

Old Comrades Brewing Company Limited was opened after WWII, and was operated from 1948 to 1953, by a group of war veterans—hence the name of the company. In 1953, it was purchased by Canadian Breweries Limited and closed in 1956. Other brands by this brewery were Old Stock Ale and Schneider's Beer.

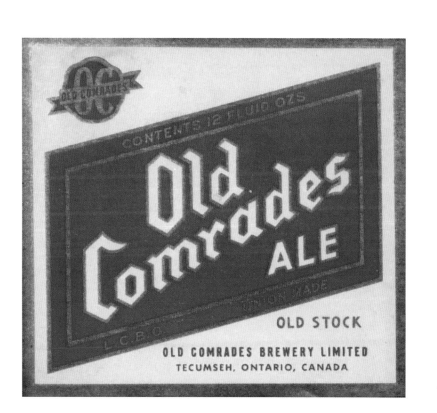

PELLER BREWING COMPANY LIMITED
Hamilton, Ontario

GOLD CROWN BEER

1950

In 1927, Andrew Peller, a native of Hungary, came to Canada and worked for various breweries in Ontario before opening the Peller Brewing Company Limited in 1946. The company prospered but could not expand since advertising was restricted by provincial regulations. Canadian Breweries acquired the plant in 1953, and Andrew went on to found Andrés Wines (now known as Peller Estates Winery). In 1988, I had the pleasure of sitting at the head table, next to Andrew, at the Canadian Brewerianist convention in Hamilton. The brewery closed and reopened several times and is now the home of Collective Arts Brewing (see page 298).

PELISSIER'S BREWERY LIMITED
Winnipeg, Manitoba

TRIPLEX STOUT XXX

1950s

Originally from Quebec, the Pelissiers moved to Manitoba in the late 1800s, where they started in the soda water business before brewing beer. The brewery operated under this name from 1939 to 1969, even though it was taken over by Shea's (60%) and Drewrys (40%) in 1936. This was a little unusual, because Shea's and Drewrys were competitors. This label, just like many drawings of breweries in the 1800s and early 1900s, embellished the size of the brewery, which was a common design convention of the time.

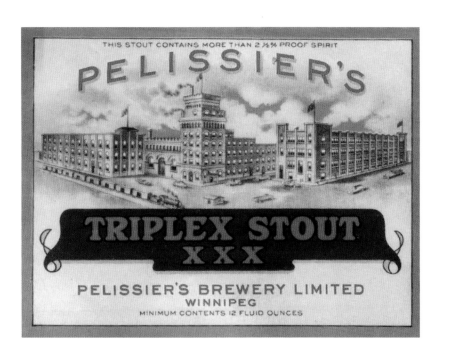

RANGER BREWING COMPANY LIMITED
Kitchener, Ontario

RANGER ALE

1950s

In 1952, the Blue Top Brewing Company in Kitchener was reorganized and named the Ranger Brewing Company Limited, with the company name taking its inspiration from the forest rangers of the region. The neck labels were an innovative design idea for the times, each carrying a different leaf of a Canadian tree. The brewery was short-lived and was purchased by Canadian Breweries Limited in 1953, and operated as the Dow Kingsbeer Brewery Limited (1953) until it was closed 1961.

THIS BREW IS MADE FROM CHOICE MALT & HOPS · MILD · TASTING AND MELLOW

CONTENTS 12 FLUID OUNCES

RANGER
ale

UNION MADE
L · C · B · O

RANGER BREWING COMPANY LTD. KITCHENER ONTARIO CANADA

HOW MANY TREES CAN YOU TELL BY THEIR LEAVES?

BEECH. *Long-pointed, oval, this leaf has sharp, slender double teeth, is 2 to 4 inches long, blue-green colour* *above; is pale green with small tufts of whitish hair that appear sometimes at the junctures of the veins underneath.*

RANGER BREWING COMPANY LTD., KITCHENER, ONT.

HOW MANY TREES CAN YOU TELL BY THEIR LEAVES?

ALDER *leaves are broad, oval and sharp-pointed— usually they are double-toothed, 1½ to 4 inches long, dull* *dark green above with conspicuous veins, smooth or hairy, with a whitish bloom on the underside.*

RANGER BREWING COMPANY LTD., KITCHENER, ONT.

HOW MANY TREES CAN YOU TELL BY THEIR LEAVES?

WILLOW *leaf alternates on either side of the branch, it is long, narrow, pointed at both ends; usually* *has fine-toothed edges, dark green above, is paler and covered with a fine down under the leaf.*

RANGER BREWING COMPANY LTD., KITCHENER, ONT.

WESTMINSTER BREWERY LIMITED
New Westminster, British Columbia

LUCKY LAGER

1950s

A brewery was established on this site as early as 1879, and the Westminster Brewery name was used from the 1880s until 1950, when it was reorganized as the Lucky Lager Brewery. This label, which predates 1960, is probably the most distinct die-cut label produced for a beer in Canada. The brand is still brewed by Labatt.

BAVARIAN BREWING COMPANY
St. John's, Newfoundland

SUMMER SPECIALS

1950s

In the fifties, these two labels were part of summer beer promotions for the Bavarian Brewing Company, which is now owned by Labatt's. An intrinsic part of Atlantic heritage, the fishing lures on the labels' design speaks to the Newfoundlanders' way of life: Jock Scott is a type of fishing fly, as is Silver Doctor. A passenger train—officially called the Caribou, and informally referred to by locals as the "Newfie Bullet"—transported fishing enthusiasts to various locations where they could indulge in their favourite pastime.

Jock Scott

SUMMER SPECIAL

Made by
BAVARIAN
BREWING LTD.
St John's
Nfld

BOARD OF LIQUOR CONTROL NEWFOUNDLAND THIS BEER CONTAINS
NOT LESS THAN 3% ALCOHOL BY VOLUME. GOVT. LICENSE № 33

Silver Doctor

SUMMER
SPECIAL

Made by
BAVARIAN
BREWING LTD.
St John's
Nfld

BOARD OF LIQUOR CONTROL NEWFOUNDLAND THIS BEER CONTAINS
NOT LESS THAN 3% ALCOHOL BY VOLUME. GOVT. LICENSE № 33

OLAND & SON LIMITED
Halifax, Nova Scotia

OLAND'S SCHOONER BEER
OLAND'S EXPORT ALE

1960

In 1960, these two vivid commemorative labels were issued by Oland & Son Limited, Brewers and Bottlers, in honour of fifty years of service by the Royal Canadian Navy. At this time, this brewery was still owned by one branch of the Oland family; it was then purchased by Labatt in 1971.

TARTAN BREWING LIMITED
Prince George, British Columbia

TARTAN PILSNER

1960s

In 1962, Tartan Brewing Limited was started in Prince George by Ben Ginter after he bought the former Cariboo Brewing Company Limited brewery, which Canadian Breweries closed in 1961. Ben had been in the contracting business, but was always up for a new challenge. He entered the brewing business using the name Tartan Brewing, featuring tartans on his labels simply because he liked tartans. His was also the first brewery in British Columbia to sell beer in cans in 1966. In 1972, he established his second brewery, Uncle Ben's Breweries of Alberta Limited, in Red Deer.

Tartan

PILSNER

BREWED WITH PURE NORTHERN SPRING WATER

TARTAN

UNCLE BEN'S

PILSNER BEER

TARTAN BREWING LIMITED
Prince George, British Columbia

HIGH LIFE

1960s

Ben Ginter often sought out marketing gimmicks for his beer, and one of his strategies was to adopt the names of some big American brands, such as High Life. Ginter's version features an artist's loose interpretation of British Columbia Coastal First Nations art on the label. On the second version of the label, we see a depiction of various aspects of beer production.

Other brands Ginter introduced included PAAPs and BUDD. However, court orders from the American breweries forced him to drop these brands. He changed the company's name to Uncle Ben's Tartan Brewery Limited in 1971.

CALGARY BREWING & MALTING COMPANY
Calgary, Alberta

STAMPEDE BEER

1967

A.E. Cross' buffalo's head and horseshoe logo made a compelling design for Calgary brands for many years. Stampede Beer was issued annually in honour of the world-renowned event that draws thousands. Shown here is the label that was issued in 1967 in celebration of the brewery's seventy-fifth anniversary. In this design, the buffalo is facing forward; earlier versions of the logo have the buffalo facing left. The signatures on the label are those of the brewery's employees.

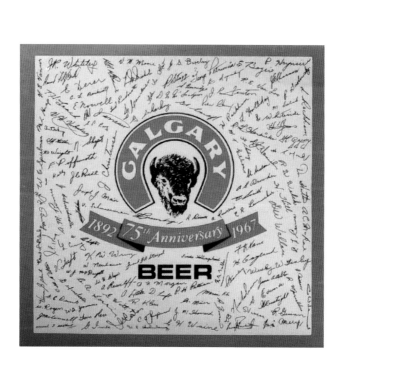

LABATT'S ALBERTA BREWERY
Edmonton, Alberta

LABATT'S PILSENER

1967

Labatt's Pilsener was introduced in 1951 and shortly went national as Labatt's Blue—with credit going to Manitobans for establishing this moniker for Labatt's Pilsener because of the blue colour of the label. Over twenty-five of these special labels were issued by Labatt's Alberta Brewery in Edmonton, Alberta, to celebrate Canada's centennial in 1967, and to promote centennial activities and events in that province—for example, encouraging customers to "Visit the Lethbridge Japanese Gardens, most authentic in North America."

O'MALLEY ALE

1968

O'Malley Ale is from the short-lived O'Malley Brewery that opened in June 1965 in Quebec City. It was established by William O'Malley, who had worked for other breweries before. It used a new continuous flow fermentation system, and only two batches were produced before the brewery closed. The beer was sold in twelve-ounce stubby bottles and the larger twenty-two-ounce quarts. This was not the end for the O'Malley name in the Canadian brewing business: in 2011 his grandson, Bryan O'Malley, and two other surfers opened Tofino Brewing Company in Tofino, British Columbia (see page 306).

THE ATLANTIC BREWING COMPANY
Stephenville, Newfoundland

ATLANTIC LAGER
ATLANTIC DRAFT

1968–1969

The Atlantic Brewing Company, established in 1968, was short-lived, closing in 1969. With a minimalist King Neptune logo and streamlined typeface, these labels convey a sophisticated visual aesthetic that is distinct for the era—especially when considering the many restrictions on advertising in the brewing industry. Because of Newfoundland's relative distance from the more urban, populated areas of Canada, it is notable that this diminutive brewery tapped into such a progressive style. Reactivated in 1971, it operated for two years as the Bison Brewing Company.

BOHEMIAN MAID BREWING COMPANY LIMITED
Edmonton, Alberta

O'KEEFE STEIN BEER

1970s

With roots that reach back to 1896, the Bohemian Maid Brewing company was thwarted by Prohibition, resulting in its closure between 1916 and 1924. Reopening in 1924, it operated as the Northwest Brewing Company until 1958, when Calgary Brewing & Malting bought control and changed the name to Bohemian Maid Brewery. The playful, heraldic-style O'Keefe Stein label dates to the early 1970s after Canadian Breweries—a conglomerate that operated Carling, O'Keefe, and Dow breweries in different provinces—had acquired Bohemian Maid in 1971.

DORAN'S NORTHERN ONTARIO BREWERIES
Sudbury, Ontario

HAW EATER'S BREW

1970s

This label declares that it's "sold only in the land of the haw eater"—Manitoulin Island—and features an interesting illustration of the region. But what are hawberries? They are berries that grow in abundance on Manitoulin Island; those who come from the prairies know them as the popular native Saskatoon berry, though berries are not an ingredient in this beer. Doran's made this brew in celebration of the unique identity of Manitoulin Island residents, and named it after them.

Barrie, Ontario

KEG DRAFT ALE

1972

This brewing company's origins date all the way back to 1869 in Formosa, Ontario, where it closed in 1970. A new Formosa brewery opened in Barrie, Ontario, in January 1972. Molson purchased the plant in 1974, and it closed in 1997.

This brand has a special place in my collection because when it was first introduced in 1974, it came in both bottles and cans. Three months later, liquor control officials made it illegal to label a beer "draft" in such containers, and the name was changed to Keg Ale. As a result, this label is rare. I purchased a twelve-pack of the Keg Draft Ale cans, one of which became the first to enter my collection.

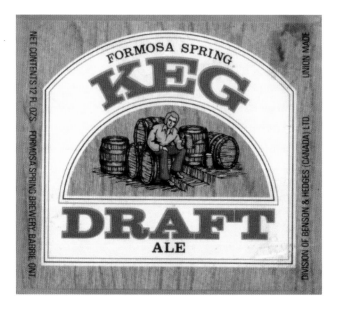

HENNINGER BREWERY (ONTARIO) LIMITED
Hamilton, Ontario

NUMBER 1 BREW LIGHT

Early 1970s

After it closed in 1960, the former Peller Brewery in Hamilton was used for other purposes. In 1974 it reopened under the Henninger name, and operated until 1981, when Heineken Group took it over and opened Amstel Brewery Canada Limited. Number 1 Brew Light was a post-WWII entry in the low-alcohol market, with only seventy-five calories per bottle. In contrast to the Prohibition era, the consumer's new demand for low-alcohol content was motivated by awareness of calorie intake—heralding the dawn of a body-conscious era that gained momentum in the early seventies and beyond.

INTERIOR BREWERIES LIMITED
Creston, British Columbia

MOUNTAIN BREW

1970s

Built in 1960, Interior Breweries Limited operated under this name until 1972 when it was purchased by Labatt and reorganized as the Columbia Brewing Company Limited. Today it is the home of Kokanee Beer. This brand, a malt liquor, would have been produced during the early 1970s.

UNCLE BEN'S BREWERIES OF ALBERTA LIMITED
Red Deer, Alberta

UNCLE BEN'S MALT LIQUOR

Early 1970s

In 1969, Ben Ginter put his own name and a picture of himself on the label and cans of Uncle Ben's Malt Liquor. He opened this brewery, his second in Red Deer, Alberta, in 1972.

BREWED WITH PURE NORTHERN SPRING WATER

UNCLE BEN'S

MALT LIQUOR

NET CONTENTS 12 FLUID OUNCES

NET CONTENTS 12 FLUID OUNCES

UNCLE BEN'S BREWERIES OF ALBERTA LTD., RED DEER, ALBERTA

UNCLE BEN'S BREWERIES OF ALBERTA LIMITED
Red Deer, Alberta

GENTLE BEN BEER

1970s

After Ben Ginter expanded into Alberta, building a new brewery in Red Deer, he also expanded his business into Manitoba with a brewery in Transcona. Once again he featured his name and image on one of the labels for Gentle Ben Beer; on the other version, we see that he chose a humourous, whimsical illustration in the spirit of Robin Hood and his Merry Men.

LA BRASSERIE MOLSON DU QUEBEC LIMITÉE
Montreal, Quebec

MOLSON BREWERIES OF CANADA LIMITED
Toronto, Ontario

LAURENTIDE ALE
CANADIAN LAGER
EXPORT ALE

1970s–1980s

From 1975 to 1988, Molson issued over 100 overprint labels. In Quebec, the labels for Molson Export and Laurentide promoted cultural and sporting events; the same was done in Ontario, on Molson Canadian labels. These labels and their stubby bottles are very collectible, but rarely seen today. The Laurentide label has the *consumption sur premises* CSP "enclosure" around the mandatory text that specifies bottle size and alcohol percentage, and was required for beer sold in taverns in Quebec at that time. However, this enclosure was not seen on the labels of beer sold in the *depanneurs*—corner stores found in every Montreal neighbourhood.

BIÈRE

FESTIVAL D'AUTOMNE DE RIMOUSKI

du 2 au 8 OCT. 1979

Laurentide

ALE

341 ml 12 oz fl 5% alc/vol

LA BRASSERIE MOLSON DU QUÉBEC LTÉE, MONTRÉAL

341 ml 12 oz fl

5% alc/vol

Folk Arts Festival

ST. CATHARINES

CENTENNIAL

May 23rd to June 6th, 1976

MOLSON

CANADIAN

BIÈRE *Lager* BEER

MOLSON BREWERIES OF CANADA LTD.

REGINA · EDMONTON · VANCOUVER

TORONTO · MONTREAL

CANADA · UNION MADE

An honest brew makes its own friends . . . John Molson

50E6 · R

1786

M

MOLSON

BIÈRE

EXPO

LA BRASSERIE MOLSON DU QUÉBEC LIMITÉE, MONTRÉAL QUÉ.

MOLSON'S BREWERY QUÉBEC · LIMITED

Grand Prix Molson Trois-Rivières

3-5 SEPT. 1976

341 ml 12 oz fl

5% alc/vol

MOOSEHEAD BREWERIES LIMITED
Saint John, New Brunswick

MOOSEHEAD EXPORT ALE

1982

The iconic Moosehead moose, which we have come to know and love, appeared as early as the 1920s on an oval label for Moosehead Pale Ale. At that time, the company was known as New Brunswick Breweries Limited; the Moosehead company name was adopted in 1947. The label for Moosehead Export Ale won the first Canadian Brewerianist Label of the Year Award for 1982.

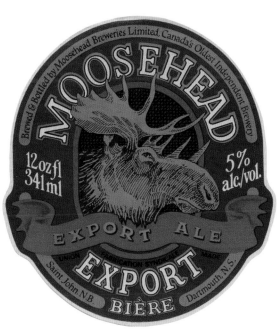

NORTHERN BREWERIES LIMITED
Sudbury, Ontario

SUPERIOR LAGER BEER

1983

With its large and unusual wraparound label, Northern Superior Lager offers an example of one of several labels designed in this graphic style used by Northern Breweries for their brands in the 1980s. At that time, Northern Breweries had plants in Sudbury, Sault Ste. Marie, Timmins, and Thunder Bay. This label won the Canadian Brewerianist Label of the Year Award for 1983.

OLAND BREWERIES LIMITED
Halifax, Nova Scotia

OLAND SCHOONER BEER

1984

Schooner Beer was first brewed by Oland in the 1950s and was named after the famous racing and fishing vessel, the schooner *Bluenose*. The latter die-cut version of the Schooner label was selected as the Canadian Brewerianist Label of the Year for 1984. In 1990, I had the opportunity to board the *Bluenose II* while in Halifax for a Canadian Brewerianist convention.

ROCKY MOUNTAIN BREWERIES LIMITED
Red Deer, Alberta

BEER

Mid-1980s

You can't get much more minimalist than this label. Rocky Mountain's Beer was produced by the Rocky Mountain Breweries, which opened in 1983, in what had been the Uncle Ben's Breweries of Alberta Limited plant. It was a low-priced contract beer produced for Blacksmith Beverages Limited in Richmond, British Columbia, in the mid-1980s.

341 ml. UNION MADE 5% alc./vol.

BeeR
BIERE

ROCKY MOUNTAIN BREWERIES LTD., RED DEER, ALTA.

ISLAND BREWERIES LIMITED
Milton, Prince Edward Island

OLD ABBY

1986–1989

Island Breweries was PEI's first modern brewery, albeit short-lived from 1986–1989. It was established by Bill Rix, who manufactured equipment for the food and brewing industries.

I was lucky to be able to visit the brewery while it was in operation. We arrived early on a Saturday and were led in by the inspector for the PEI Alcohol Commission, who happened to be there that day. "Bill won't be in until noon," he told us, and he invited us to go into the hospitality room to have an Island beer. We eventually had the opportunity to meet Bill and talk with him about brewing beer on Prince Edward Island.

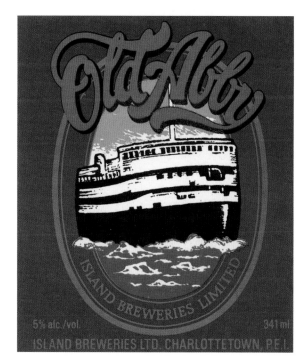

ISLAND BREWERIES LIMITED

5% alc./vol.   341 ml

ISLAND BREWERIES LTD. CHARLOTTETOWN, P.E.I.

LA BRASSERIE O'KEEFE LIMITÉE
Montreal, Quebec
CARLING O'KEEFE BREWERIES
Toronto, Ontario

LA BIÈRE BERNARD HAYS
WALLY CROUTER BEER

1986

La Brasserie O'Keefe Limitée and Carling-O'Keefe Breweries, produced special labels to honour various people at important milestones in their lives. Bernard Hays worked in the Montreal brewery office as company archivist and special assistant to the president, and was a great supporter of all Canadian breweriana collectors. Other labels were issued for special events to honour Canadians—for example, Toronto's mayor Mel Lastman, Wally Crouter from CFRB radio in Toronto (in honour of his retirement in 1996), and other noteworthy individuals.

AMSTEL BREWERY CANADA LIMITED
Hamilton, Ontario

GRIZZLY CANADIAN LAGER

1987

Heineken purchased the Henninger Brewery (Ontario) in 1981—its first brewery in North America. Amstel, owned by Heineken, produced various local brands, such as Steeler, Hamilton Mountain Beer, Laker, and Laker Light. Produced for both the Ontario and American markets, promotional material included a statuette of a bear on a tree stump holding a beer bottle. In the US, the grizzly bear motif was viewed as quintessentially Canadian, and in Canada, the label won the Canadian Brewerianist Label of the Year Award for 1987. Amstel Brewery Canada was reorganized as Lakeport Brewery Corporation in 1992 and was eventually bought by Labatt.

HIGHLAND BREWERIES
Sydney, Nova Scotia

HIGHLAND CLASSIC ALE

1987–1989

This was Nova Scotia's first, but short-lived, microbrewery, operating in Sydney from 1987–1990. It followed shortly after the launch of Nova Scotia's first brewpub, Gingers, opened by Kevin Keefe in Halifax in 1985. This label lives up to its name with its undeniable East Coast spirit, and the design concept clearly honours the island known for its talented fiddlers.

Quality ale

BIÈRE HIGHLAND ALE

HIGHLAND BREWERIES

341 ml CLASSIC 5% alc./vol.

"CAPE BRETON'S OWN!"

SYDNEY NOVA SCOTIA CANADA

NIAGARA FALLS BREWING COMPANY
Niagara Falls, Ontario

TRAPPER LAGER

1989

The Niagara Falls Brewing Company was established in 1989.
In July of that year, the company introduced its Trapper Lager
and won the Canadian Brewerianist Label of the Year Award for
1989. This brewery was taken over by Moosehead, and production was moved to Brampton in 2004, where it is now known
as Hop City Brewing Company. The label's artwork captures
the much-loved spirit of the iconic, intrepid Canadian trapper.

Niagara

·Trapper·

PREMIUM CANADIAN

LAGER

Beer   Bière

5% alc./vol.   341 mL

Brewed and Bottled By Niagara Falls Brewing Company, Niagara Falls, Ontario, Canada

O'BRUNSWICK MALT LIQUOR

Late 1980s

Hanshaus Brewery (also known as Bavarian Specialties Canada) was New Brunswick's first modern microbrewery, but it only operated from 1986 to 1991. This bold label festooned a 780 mL bottle of a 6.0% malt liquor. Hanshaus was an early adopter of five-litre kegs, and I had the pleasure of seeing them filled during a visit to the brewery.

COTTAGE BREWERY

BAVARIAN PURITY LAW OF 1516

Hanshaus

LIQUEUR de MALT LIQUOR

O'Brunswick

Traditionally
Brewed

Brassée
traditionnellement

BREWMASTER
GUARANTEED

PRODUCT OF CANADA   PRODUIT DU CANADA

+908780

780 ml

BAVARIAN SPECIALTIES (CANADA) LTD.
DIEPPE, N.B., CANADA

6.0% Alc./Vol.

LABATT BREWING COMPANY LIMITED
London, Ontario

LABATT'S BLUE

1992

Issued in 1992, this label for Labatt's Blue honours the fifteenth anniversary of Labatt moving into what was originally the Kuntz Brewery, which was first established on that site in 1840. Labatt purchased the brewery from Carling O'Keefe in 1977, and it was eventually closed in 1992—the same year of the release of this label.

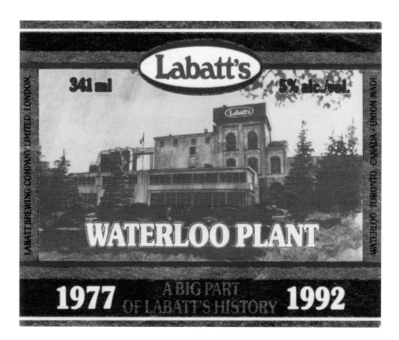

SILVER CREEK BREWERY COMPANY LIMITED
Guelph, Ontario

ARCTIC WOLF BEER

1993

The revitalized Sleeman Brewing Company introduced this beer under the old Silver Creek Brewery name, which was used pre-Prohibition. This distinct label for its Arctic Wolf Beer won the Canadian Brewerianist Label of the Year Award for 1993.

ARCTIC WOLF

The beer with the
Arctic fresh taste

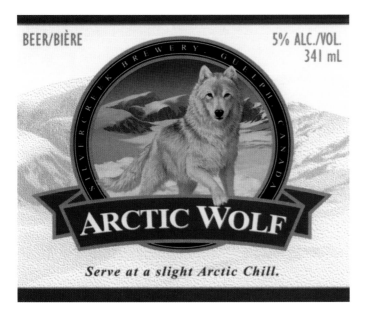

BEER/BIÈRE

5% ALC./VOL.
341 mL

SILVERCREEK BREWERY · GUELPH · CANADA

ARCTIC WOLF

Serve at a slight Arctic Chill.

ARCTIC WOLF

Une bière d'une qualité sans compromis, "Arctic Wolf"
est brassée en petites quantités dans des bouilloires
de cuivre, à partir d'ingrédients tous naturels afin de lui
donner un goût unique, riche et rafraîchissant.

A beer of uncompromising quality, Arctic Wolf is
brewed in small batches in copper kettles using
all natural ingredients, to deliver a taste that's uniquely
rich and refreshing. Serve at a slight Arctic Chill.

LABATT BREWING COMPANY LIMITED
London, Ontario

LABATT 50 D-DAY COMMEMORATIVE BREW

1994

In 1994, this Labatt 50 D-Day Commemorative Brew marked the fiftieth anniversary of D-Day. It won the Canadian Brewerianist Label of the Year Award for 1994, with subtle yet riveting artwork that honoured those who served their country.

BREW BROTHERS BREWING COMPANY LIMITED
Calgary, Alberta

PRAIRIE STEAM ALE

1997

Established in 1994 by five home brewers from Newfoundland, Brew Brothers opened its own craft brewery in Calgary. After nineteen years of creativity and collaboration, the brewery closed down. The characters on this label are the likenesses of the individuals who participated in the founding of this endeavour. Prairie Steam Ale was the winner of the Canadian Brewerianist Label of the Year Award for 1997.

HANDCRAFTED

BREW BROTHERS
BREWING COMPANY LIMITED

CALGARY · ALBERTA

+686311   2-H-15

PRAIRIE
STEAM
ALE

6.5%
alc.vol.

1000
ml.

BREW BROTHERS BREWING COMPANY LIMITED

SPECIAL
EDITION

RETURN FOR DEPOSIT WHERE APPLICABLE

BEER · BIÈRE · CALGARY, ALBERTA, CANADA

MOLSON BREWERIES
St. John's, Newfoundland and Labrador

BLACK HORSE CAPE SPEAR
BLACK HORSE GROS MORNE

1997

Black Horse beer originated with the Dawes Black Horse Brewery, which dates back to 1811 in Lachine, Quebec, later moving to Montreal. Several changes in ownership ensued until Carling O'Keefe merged with Molson in 1989. Today, Black Horse is produced exclusively at Molson's St. John's plant.

Issued in 1997 to promote Newfoundland's heritage, these labels are only two of at least twelve different ones that I acquired by soaking the labels off bottles while in St. John's in September 1997. One features Cape Spear, the easternmost part of Canada, and the other shows Gros Morne National Park on the west coast of Newfoundland.

BLACK HORSE

BREWED FOR YOU ON:

16SEP97

FOR PRODUCT
INFORMATION CALL:
1-800-MOLSON1

FRESHEST TASTE
WITHIN 110 DAYS

BLACK HORSE

THE UNOFFICIAL BREW OF CABOT'S CREW

BLACK HORSE

THE UNOFFICIAL BREW OF CABOT'S CREW

BIG ROCK BREWERY
Calgary, Alberta

CHINOOK DRY
HOPPED PALE ALE

1998

Founded in Calgary, Alberta, in 1985, Big Rock Brewery was
named after a large glacial rock near Okotoks, eighteen kilo-
metres south of Calgary. They continue to brew a large range
of craft beers to this date, operating three brewery locations
in Calgary, Vancouver, and Toronto. Chinook Dry Hopped Pale
Ale has been discontinued, but not before leaving an admi-
rable legacy: it won the Canadian Brewerianist Label of the
Year Award for 1998, and partnered with the Pacific Salmon
Foundation, donating a portion from each sale of Chinook Dry
Hopped Pale Ale to salmon conservation—hence the salmon
on the label.

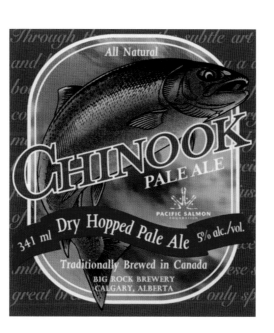

All Natural

CHINOOK
PALE ALE

PACIFIC SALMON
FOUNDATION

341 ml Dry Hopped Pale Ale 5% alc./vol.

Traditionally Brewed in Canada

BIG ROCK BREWERY
CALGARY, ALBERTA

THE GREAT WESTERN BREWING COMPANY LIMITED
Saskatoon, Saskatchewan

SASKATCHEWAN BEER

1998

The origins of the Great Western Brewing Company date all the way back to the Hub City Brewing Company, founded in 1927. In 1952 it was purchased by Canadian Breweries Limited, and for several years was a unit of the O'Keefe Brewing Company. After Carling O'Keefe merged with Molson, the plant became redundant and was sold to a group of employees in 1989, only to be resurrected as the Great Western Brewing Company in 1990, still an independent brewery today. This is its Saskatchewan Beer, nicknamed "Saskie Beer."

5% alc./vol. • 341 ml • Beer / Bière

SASKATCHEWAN BEER

NO PRESERVATIVES · NATURALLY AGED

We would like to hear your comments 1-800-764-4492
Crafted with care by
The Great Western Brewing Company Limited
Saskatoon, Canada · Union Made · Return For Refund

Fredericton, New Brunswick

SIMEON JONES RIVER VALLEY AMBER ALE

1998

In 1995, Picaroons opened in Fredericton, New Brunswick. Simeon Jones River Valley Amber Ale was first brewed in 1998 for the King's Head Inn and King's Landing, and was the first beer to be bottled in Picaroons' 500 mL bottles; it is still brewed today. Simeon Jones himself dates back to 1848 in Saint John, where he was employed by Robert Keltie, who had a brewery there. Simeon later purchased the brewery. While there is no direct connection between Simeon Jones and Picaroons, the modern-day brewing company wanted to resurrect the Simeon Jones Amber Ale as Simeon Jones was a historic New Brunswick figure.

**Beer
500ml**

Born in 1828, Simeon Jones was raised on a farm in
the St. John River Valley. As a young man he moved
to Saint John, where he eventually established a
brewery which became known throughout the
Maritimes for its hearty, robust, amber ale

In addition to being a keen businessman, Jones was
mayor of Saint John. Always a gentleman, he was
respected for his generosity, charity and kindness.
You can visit his childhood home at Kings Landing
Historical Settlement, located west of Fredericton,
New Brunswick (see www.kingslanding.nb.ca).

This fine ale is brewed in the tradition of Simeon
Jones by the Northampton Brewing Company.

Return for refund where applicable

**Bière
4.5% alc./vol.**

Né en 1828, Simeon Jones a grandi sur une ferme
dans la vallée du fleuve Saint-Jean. Jeune homme,
il se rend à Saint John, où il établit éventuellement une
brasserie qui devient alors connue partout dans les
Maritimes pour son ale ambrée au goût
franc et corsé.

En plus d'être un bon homme d'affaires, Jones est élu
maire de Saint John. Gentilhomme, il s'attire le respect
par sa générosité, sa bienveillance et sa charité. Vous
pouvez visiter sa maison d'enfance au Village historique
de Kings Landing, situé à l'ouest de Fredericton, au
Nouveau-Brunswick (voir : www.kingslanding.nb.ca).

Cette bière de grande qualité est fabriquée dans la
tradition de Simeon Jones par la Northampton
Brewing Company.

Consigné là où la loi le prescrit

MT. BEGBIE BREWING COMPANY
Revelstoke, British Columbia

HIGH COUNTRY KÖLSCH

Late 1990s

Mt. Begbie Brewing Company used old black and white histori-cal photographs for its early labels, evoking a pleasant sense of nostalgia. In this example, the label features a 1929 picture of the Falcons, a Revelstoke hockey team, after its victory at the Tri-City Championship. Other brands featured pictures from the BC Archives and the Revelstoke Archives. A more recent Kölsch label featured another photograph of a steam engine—again from the Revelstoke Archives. More recent labels, such as those on bottles of Nasty Habit, have featured exotic artwork.

High Country Kölsch

The Joy of Thirst.

"The Falcons" hockey team, Revelstoke, 1931-33

+688929

6 29216 88929 4

Brewed right here in the spectacular Columbias, this pale German-style Kölschbier is a real thirst quencher. No preservatives or additives.

4.5% alc./vol. beer

650 ml

Refrigerate after purchase

Mt. Begbie Brewing Company, Revelstoke, BC

Box 2995, 207 Victoria Rd. East, Revelstoke, BC V0E 2S0 CANADA

Mt. Begbie Brewing Co. Revelstoke BC

QUIDI VIDI BREWERY
St. John's, Newfoundland and Labrador

ICEBERG BEER

Late 1990s

Quidi Vidi Brewery was established in 1996 in a former fishing plant on the water's edge in the Quidi Vidi fishing village, a neighbourhood of St. John's, Newfoundland. It is located in what I consider to be one of the most picturesque locations for a brewery in Canada. One distinct brand the brewery produces is Iceberg Beer, a unique beer made from water harvested from icebergs that drift off the coast of Newfoundland, which is less than a kilometre away.

ICEBERG ®

BEER • BIERE

Made with pure 25,000 year old iceberg water

QUIDI VIDI BREWERY

ST. JOHN'S, NL, CANADA

www.icebergbeer.com

341 ml
Pry-off Crown

4.5% alc/vol.

Return for refund where applicable

YUKON GOLD

1999

This first modern brewery in the Yukon was opened in 1997 as the Chilkoot Brewing Company Limited in Whitehorse, but later changed its name to the Yukon Brewing Company. This version of its popular Yukon Gold won the Canadian Brewerianist Label of the Year Award for 1999.

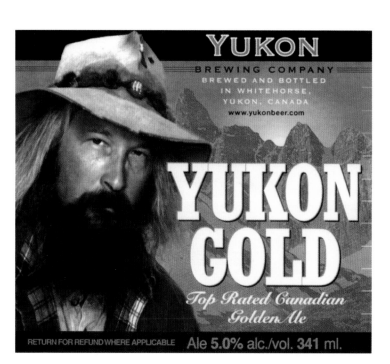

BRASSERIE VIEUX-MONTRÉAL (BVM)
Montreal, Quebec

VIEUX-MONTRÉAL RED BEER

2000

When walking along the cobblestone streets and historic buildings of Old Montreal, you'll find Brasserie Vieux-Montréal, which started brewing under the official name of Brasserie BVM. "Brewed in accordance with the Bavarian Purity Law of 1516," as its website proclaims, its beers are now available exclusively in cans and on draught. The label and neck band from its early bottles evoke the romantic imagery of the Old Port and *les calèches* (horse-drawn carriages) of days gone by.

BIÈRE
ROUSSE

RED
BEER

Vieux-Montréal

BIÈRE ROUSSE
RED BEER

ALE

5% alc./vol.   341mL

INGRÉDIENTS: EAU, LEVURE, HOUBLON, MALT.
INGREDIENTS: WATER, YEAST, HOPS, MALT.

RETOURNER POUR REMBOURSEMENT LÀ OÙ IL Y A LIEU.
RETURN FOR REFUND WHERE APPLICABLE.

LES BRASSERIES BVM DU CANADA,
MONTRÉAL (QUÉBEC) CANADA H2V 4P9

La bière Vieux-Montréal est une bière de qualité supérieure brassée par des maîtres-brasseurs qui ont à cœur de produire une bière parfaite. Cette bière rousse tout à fait unique est brassée en petites quantités et livrée à nos clients délicieusement fraîche; à chaque semaine. Chaque brassage, effectué consciencieusement à la Loi bavaroise de la pureté de 1516, contient quatre ingrédients, de l'eau, du malt d'orge de premier choix, des houblons importés et une levure spéciale.

Vieux-Montréal premium ales handcrafted by a team of brewmasters dedicated to producing the perfect beer. This unique beer ale is brewed in small batches and delivered fresh weekly to each one of our customers. Every batch contains four ingredients; water, select barley malt, imported hops and our unique yeast, and is brewed in accordance with the Bavarian Purity Law of 1516.

STEAM WHISTLE BREWING COMPANY
Toronto, Ontario

PREMIUM PILSNER

2000

Steam Whistle Brewing Company was founded in 2000 when a new brewery was built in the historic John Street Roundhouse, just south of the CN Tower in Toronto. This unique green glass bottle is decorated with a distinctive painted label, also known as an applied ceramic label. The design is essentially the same today, except for minor changes made over the years, and guaranteed to attract the attention of serious collectors of Canadian beer bottles. Steam Whistle has only brewed one beer—Premium Pilsner—since day one.

UNIBROUE
Chambly, Quebec

LA BOLDUC

2000

Unibroue started when its founders purchased La Brasserie Massawippi in 1991 in Lennoxville, Quebec. They then established a new brewery in Chambly in 1993, and have since produced an extensive variety of bottled beers—including an old-style beer called La Bolduc—featuring a series of early Quebec scenes on the labels. There was also a series of the same pictures on eighteen different five-litre mini-kegs, which are called "cans" by breweriana collectors.

341mL   5% alc./vol.

L_A BOLDUC

Bière à l'ancienne • Old style Beer

Place du Marché, Joliette
1911

1/9

UNIBROUE
CHAMBLY QUÉBEC CANADA

MANO'S GRILL AND BREWHOUSE
Saskatoon, Saskatchewan

WHITE BISON
SMOOTH PALE ALE

2003

Mano's Grill and Brewhouse opened in Saskatoon in 1981. This large and colourful label for its White Bison Smooth Pale Ale won the Canadian Brewerianist Society Label of the Year Award for 2003. Mano's now sells a beer called Canadian Wildlife in a 355 mL can. While attending a Canadian Brewerianist convention in Saskatoon, I had the privilege of filling and personally capping my own can of Mano's beer.

mano's

2.0 L

8.0%
ALC./VOL.

WHITE BISON
SMOOTH PALE ALE

NO ADDITIVES OR PRESERVATIVES · MANO'S · 2202 · 22nd STREET WEST · (306) 683-3333

CANADIAN WILD LIFE BEER
SASKATOON SASKATCHEWAN

TWO RIVERS BREWING
Winnipeg, Manitoba

TWO RIVERS RED

2004

Two Rivers Brewing was originally established in Winnipeg in 1997, but merged with Fort Garry Brewing Company Limited in 2003. Two Rivers Red was retained as a brand name, and this label, which celebrates the junction of the Assiniboine and Red rivers, won the Canadian Brewerianist Society's Label of the Year Award for 2004.

NO PRESERVATIVES
CRAFT BREWED
COLD FILTERED

TWO RIVERS
BREWING

BIÈRE   MANITOBA   BEER

TWO RIVERS RED

THE FORKS

PROUDLY MADE IN MANITOBA

341 ml
5.0% alc./vol.

FORT GARRY BREWING COMPANY LTD., WINNIPEG, MANITOBA

BOSWELL STRONG DARK ALE

2006

In 1998, this farm brewery opened near the village of Saint-Germain de Kamouraska, gently nestled near the south shore of the St. Lawrence River. As the winner of the Canadian Brewerianist Society Label of the Year Award for 2006, Boswell Strong Dark Ale resurrected the Boswell name, which hearkens back to one of Quebec City's original breweries. During a trip to the east coast, I visited the brewery and was treated like royalty by Bruno Baekelmans, who was the maître brasseur (brewmaster) while the brewery was still active.

Brasserie Breughel
68, Route 132
St-Germain de
Kamouraska
(Québec) G0L 3G0
Tél: 418-492-3693
www.breughel.com

30 cents
refund
consigne

BOSWELL

INGRÉDIENTS:
eau de source, malt
d'orge, sucre de canne
biologique, coriandre,
levure haute. Aromatisée
avec houblon.

BRASSÉE SANS:
bentonite, silicates, sel,
peroxyde d'hydrogène,
agents correcteurs ni
ajusteurs de pH.

INGREDIENTS:
spring water, barley
malt, coriander,
organic cane sugar,
high-fermenting yeast.
Flavored with hops.

DOES NOT CONTAIN:
bentonite, silicates,
salt, hydrogen peroxide,
or pH correcting agents.

Bière Brune Forte   500 ml   Strong Dark Ale
                          7.5% alc. / vol.

8 15126 00049 6

PADDOCK WOOD BREWING COMPANY
Saskatoon, Saskatchewan

606 INDIA PALE ALE

2007

Paddock Wood was Saskatchewan's first microbrewery. It was established in December 1994 after it finally obtained a license to sell its beer through the Saskatchewan Liquor and Gaming Authority. As with many Canadian microbreweries, it was a fight to have archaic brewing laws changed. The 606 India Pale Ale label won the Canadian Brewerianist Society's Label of the Year Award for 2007 and is still the brewery's most popular beer.

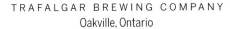

TRAFALGAR BREWING COMPANY
Oakville, Ontario

WORKER'S BROWN ALE
SOVEREIGN ALE

2007

Trafalgar Brewing Company was established in Oakville, Ontario, in 1993 and currently brews a range of ales, lagers, porters, meads, and makes beer for Black Creek Pioneer Village in Toronto. In 2013 it also established Trafalgar Artisanal Distillery to make spirits ranging from vodkas and specialty whiskies to unique moonshine and liqueurs.

Trafalgar has produced numerous unique labels, including a series of candidates pictured in various local elections in Oakville, Toronto, and London, Ontario. Here we see one for Jack Layton in the federal elections of 2006 and 2008, and another of Gilles Duceppe, former leader of the Bloc Quebecois Party.

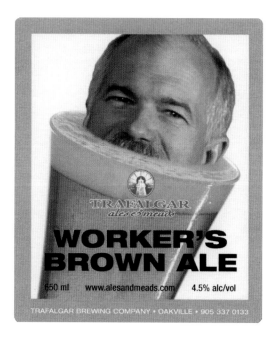

WORKER'S BROWN ALE

650 ml   www.alesandmeads.com   4.5% alc/vol

TRAFALGAR BREWING COMPANY • OAKVILLE • 905 337 0133

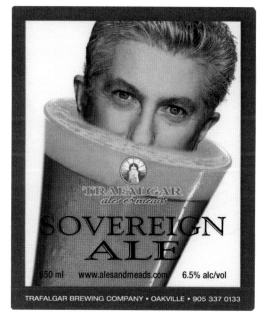

SOVEREIGN ALE

650 ml   www.alesandmeads.com   6.5% alc/vol

TRAFALGAR BREWING COMPANY • OAKVILLE • 905 337 0133

À L'ABRI DE LA TEMPÊTE MICROBRASSERIE
L'Étang-du-Nord, Quebec

ÉCUME BIERE DES ILES

2008

Located in L'Étang-du-Nord, Quebec, on the Îles de la Madeleine—one of my favourite places in Canada—this brewery is in a former fish processing plant. Founded in 2004, its name means "shelter from the storm." Les Îles (the islands) are a five-hour ferry ride from Souris, PEI, or can be reached by air or on cruise ships out of Montreal. Écume Biere des Iles, which I had the privilege of sampling when I visited the islands in 2008, is one of the brewery's first beers.

ÉCUME
BIERE DES ILES

Bière / Beer
341 ml
alc./vol.
4.8%

Il pousse aux Îles de la Madeleine la meilleure orge qui soit. À partir de ces céréales, battues par les vents et l'air salin, nous concoctons un malt aux accents maritimes qui confère à nos bières un profil gustatif unique. Située en bord de mer, la microbrasserie **À l'abri de la Tempête** vous invite à goûter la mer et son «Écume».

The best barley of all grows on the Magdalen Islands. We harvest the windblown, salt-kissed grains and use them to concoct a malt with a maritime accent that gives our beers their unique character. Come to our microbrewery **À l'abri de la Tempête** relax by the sea shore and dip your lips in a brew as fine as spindrift.

À l'abri de la
TEMPÊTE
Microbrasserie

266 ch. Coulombe
l'Étang-du-Nord, Québec
www.alabridelatempete.com

Embouteillée le / Bottled since   Année / Year
J F M A M J J A S O N D   07 08 09 10   1 2 3 4 5 6 7 8 9 10

GAHAN BREWERY
Charlottetown, PEI

SIR JOHN A'S
HONEY WHEAT ALE

2008

Established in Charlottetown in March of 1997, Gahan Brewery was originally known as Murphy's Brewing Company. After moving from its original location, it settled into its current home in Old Charlottetown, known as the birthplace of Confederation. In 2000 the Gahan Brewery name was adopted, and in July of 2008, this label for Sir John A's Honey Wheat Ale was released. The likeness of Sir John A. MacDonald is most appropriate and well chosen: he was the first prime minister of Canada and one of the Fathers of Confederation.

THE GAHAN HOUSE

BREWERY

A light golden brew with honey-ish notes on the nose and a rounded, off dry and slightly citrusy body

Murphy Group
of Restaurants
P R O D U C T

KEEP REFRIGERATED.
Return for refund where applicable.

BEER
4.5%/vol

GAHAN BREWING COMPANY

★ ★

SIR JOHN A's

HONEY WHEAT ALE

★ **HANDCRAFTED** ★
IN CHARLOTTETOWN, PRINCE EDWARD ISLAND

PRINCE EDWARD ISLAND'S ONLY BREWERY

500 ml

INGREDIENTS

Gahan Brewery Handcrafted Ales are brewed the old fashioned way using 100% natural ingredients - malted barley, hops, water and yeast - with no additives, no preservatives, and no pasteurization.

6 29261 00002 6

www.gahanbrewery.com

MISSION SPRINGS BREWING COMPANY
Mission, British Columbia

BOMBSHELL BLONDE ALE

2008

Mission Springs Brewing Company opened in October 1996 on a site that overlooks the Fraser River in Mission, British Columbia. The pub is full of collectibles, antiques, and memorabilia, and old signs and furnishings cover the walls. In the spirit of celebrating an era gone by, the style of the Bombshell Blonde Ale label hearkens back to the years of WWII. Bombshell Blonde Ale won the Collectors of Canadian Brewery Advertising (CCBA) Label of the Year Award for 2008.

Mildly Hopped & Very Refreshing!

Bombshell

Blonde

★ **ALE** ★

Ale
650 ml

Ale
4.5% alc./vol.

**MISSION
SPRINGS**
BREWING COMPANY

A lighter style Ale, mildly hopped and very refreshing. *Gentlemen Prefer Blondes!*
Ingredients: Water, Malted Barley, Hops, Yeast.
Ingrédients: l'eau, orge maltée, houblon, levure.
No additives or Preservatives • Sans additifs ou preservatifs

Brewed for you on: Month 1 2 3 4 5 6 7 8 9 10 11 12 Week 12 3 4

BRASSERIE DIEU DU CIEL!
Montreal, Quebec

CORNE DU DIABLE

2010

Brasserie Dieu du Ciel! opened a brewpub in Montreal in 1998, and since that day has produced many distinct labels. Here we have Corne du Diable (Devil's Horn), an India Pale Ale that dates from 2010. Dieu du Ciel!'s illustrated labels are so distinct that they are immediately recognizable, and are widely lauded as works of art in their own right. Dieu du Ciel! is the French version of the expletive, "Oh my God!" and is a wickedly delightful addition to its series of hedonistic labels.

Brasserie
Dieu du Ciel !

Corne du diable

Embouteillée le / Bottled on : | 01 | 02 | 03 | 04 | 05 | 06 | 07 | 08 | 09 | 10 | 11 | 12 | • | 12 | 13 | 14 | 15 |

La Corne du diable est une interprétation contemporaine des «India Pale Ales» anglaises. Ce nouveau style, né sur la côte ouest de l'Amérique du Nord, se caractérise par des bières plus fortes et beaucoup plus houblonnées. Il en résulte une bière rousse, ronde et caramélisée, qui prévient une amertume tranchante et des arômes puissants dus à un houblonnage à froid.

Ingrédients : Eau, orge maltée, blé, houblons, levure
Ingredients : Water, malted barley, wheat, hops, yeast

India pale ale
6,5 % alc./vol.

Bière forte
Strong beer
341 mL

Pour déguster toute la gamme de nos bières en fût, visitez nos deux pubs :
• 29 Laurier Ouest, Montréal, 514-490-9555 • 259 rue de Villemure, St-Jérôme, 450-436-3438
Brassée et embouteillée par / Brewed and bottled by :
Microbrasserie Dieu du Ciel inc., St-Jérôme, Québec, Canada, J7Z 5J4.
www.dieuduciel.com — infomicro@dieuduciel.com
Illustration : Yannick Brosseau — yannbrosseau@gmail.com

| 01 | 2 | 3 | 4 | 5 | 6 | 7 | 8 | 9 | • | 01 | 2 | 3 | 4 | 5 | 6 | 7 | 8 | 9 |

89076 12668

NIAGARA COLLEGE TEACHING BREWERY
Niagara-on-the-Lake, Ontario

BUTLER'S BITTER

2010

Niagara College's teaching brewery, Canada's first, was established on its Niagara-on-the-Lake campus in 2010. Since then, the brewery has been selling beers—first in growlers, then in labelled bottles. As of 2016, their beers are available in a series of twelve cans, each with a different style of beer (e.g., ale, lager, porter, etc.). The original labelled bottles were for its First Draft Campus Lager and Campus Ale, followed by a Brewmaster series. Butler's Bitter was released in 2012 in honour of the 200th anniversary of the War of 1812.

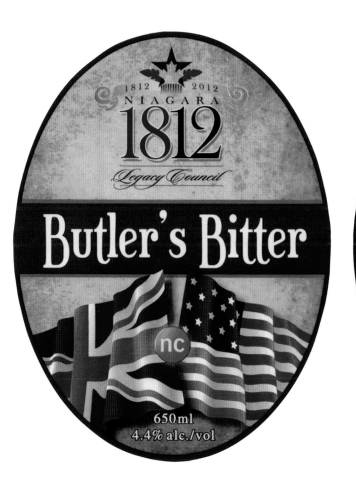

1812 — 2012

NIAGARA

1812

Legacy Council

Butler's Bitter

650ml
4.4% alc./vol

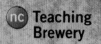 **Teaching Brewery**

Butler's Bitter

Charge your glasses with the drink that fuelled the British armies in 1812. This traditional recipe, light bodied, smooth drinking, English style Bitter has a copper brown colouring, a floral/roasted malt scent and a taste of rye bread and black coffee. Raise a glass to 200 years of peace.

Our Story

Beer and Education - a pairing that has been fermenting for generations. We've put our heads together to craft something truly unique, the Niagara College Teaching Brewery. Just like our beer, it's the only one of its kind. It's our Butler's Bitter.

Beer • Bière
650ml • 4.4% ALC./VOL.

niagaracollege.ca

PLEASE DRINK AND RECYCLE RESPONSIBLY

Niagara College Learning Enterprises Corporation 135 Taylor Road, Niagara-on-the-Lake, Ontario, Canada L0S 1J0

 PROCEEDS OF SALES SUPPORT
STUDENT LEARNING

PHILLIPS BREWING COMPANY
Victoria, British Columbia

TRAINWRECK BARLEY WINE

2011

Phillips Brewing Company opened in Esquimalt, British Columbia in 2001 and moved to a larger facility in Victoria in 2008. It has produced many creative and attractive labels for its beers; this label, with its distinctive art deco style, won the CCBA Label of the Year Award for 2011.

PHILLIPS BREWING COMPANY

TRAINWRECK

BARLEY WINE
2011

10% ALC/VOL 650mL

+797647

INGREDIENTS: WATER, MALTED BARLEY, HOPS AND YEAST

HERE'S A LITTLE SOMETHING TO STOKE YOUR BOILER. THIS BARLEY WINE IS FULL OF RICH MALT FLAVOURS AND DEEP CARAMEL AROMAS. MILDLY CARBONATED, TRAINWRECK SHOULD BE SERVED AT CELLAR TEMPERATURE (8C). CAREFUL NOT TO DERAIL YOUR CABOOSE.

PHILLIPSBEER.COM

BREWED & BOTTLED BY PHILLIPS BREWING CO. 2010 GOVERNMENT ST, VICTORIA, BC

GREAT LAKES BREWERY
Etobicoke, Ontario

LAKE EFFECT IPA

2013

In 1987, the Great Lakes Brewing Company first opened in Brampton with two beers: Great Lakes Lager and Unicorn Ale. In 1992, the brewery moved to Etobicoke and built a larger facility, and focused on Great Lakes Lager. The first 473 mL cans were unveiled in 2006 and the company has since produced over one hundred differently designed cans, much to the delight of Canadian beer can collectors—and non-collectors too. In 2013, shrink wrap label sleeves were introduced, which greatly reduce the cost of packaging beer in cans. The artwork on this series of labels is spectacular.

COLLECTIVE ARTS BREWING
Hamilton, Ontario

RANSACK THE UNIVERSE IPA
RHYME & REASON EPA
SAINT OF CIRCUMSTANCE BLONDE ALE

2014

The first Collective Arts beers were produced at Nickel Brook in Burlington, but are now brewed in the re-equipped Peller brewery, originally built in 1945 in Hamilton, Ontario. The brewery's labels feature the talent of emerging artists, musicians, and filmmakers from Canada, the United States, Asia, and Europe. Through augmented reality technology, all labels come to life via a phone app. Simply scan a label on a bottle to hear music, see videos, and view artists' bios. The sixth series of labels was released in May 2016. Many of the artist's designs have also been used on Collective Arts' coasters and beer cans.

COLLECTIVE ARTS

RANSACK *THE UNIVERSE*

HEMISPHERE IPA

Art: Dan Springer, Toronto, ON, Canada

SERIES 5
NO. 65

★
CA
BREWED IN
HAMILTON

HOPS
GALAXY
Victoria, AUS
MOSAIC
Yakima, WA

LIMITED
EDITION
LABELS

SUPPORTING
EMERGING
ARTISTS &
MUSICIANS

Scan the art.
Download the
Blippar app

355 mL
6.8% alc./vol.
STRONG BEER
BIÈRE FORTE

BREWED BY
COLLECTIVE ARTS
BREWING LIMITED,
HAMILTON, ONTARIO

To Connect or Submit Art
collectiveartsbrewing.com

1 86360 00021 5

Cait Maloney, Columbia, SC, USA
collectiveartsbrewing.com/series-3

no. 8 | Series 3

COLLECTIVE ARTS

RHYME & REASON

EXTRA PALE ALE

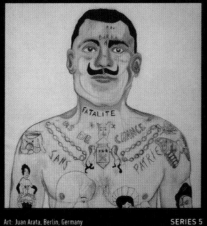

Art: Juan Arata, Berlin, Germany

SERIES 5
NO. 32

★
CA
BREWED IN
HAMILTON

HOPS
CITRA
CENTENNIAL
CHINOOK
& SIMCOE

LIMITED
EDITION
LABELS

SUPPORTING
EMERGING
ARTISTS &
MUSICIANS

Scan the art.
Download the
Blippar app

355 mL
5.7% alc./vol.
STRONG BEER
BIÈRE FORTE

BREWED BY
COLLECTIVE ARTS
BREWING LIMITED,
HAMILTON, ONTARIO

To Connect or Submit Art
collectiveartsbrewing.com

1 86360 00001 7

COLLECTIVE ARTS

SAINT *OF* CIRCUMSTANCE

CITRUS-INFUSED
BLONDE ALE

INGREDIENTS | INGRÉDIENTS:
WATER, BARLEY MALT, WHEAT MALT, HOPS, YEAST. ORANGE & LEMON
EAU, MALT D'ORGE, MALT DE BLÉ, HOUBLON, LEVURE. ORANGE ET
DE CITRON. AVERTISSEMENT D'ALLERGIE: CONTIENT DU BLÉ
ALLERGY WARNING: CONTAINS WHEAT

355 mL
4.7% alc./vol.
BEER BIÈRE

COLLECTIVE ARTS BREWING LIMITED
BURLINGTON & TORONTO, ONTARIO
collectiveartsbrewing.com

1 86360 00006 2

MILL STREET BREWERY
Toronto, Ontario

DISTILLERY ALE

2014

Mill Street Brewery opened in December 2002 in Toronto's historic Distillery District, and Organic Lager was the first beer it made. Distillery Ale was brewed to commemorate the 2013 opening of the Toronto Distillery District Beer Hall, where the Mill Street Bierschnapps is made; Distillery Ale went on to win the CCBA Label of the Year Award for 2014. The Distillery District incorporates the site of the famed Gooderham & Worts Distillery, which operated continuously for 153 years until its closure in 1990. Much of my early Toronto beer memorabilia was photographed in 2006 and is still on display at the brewpub.

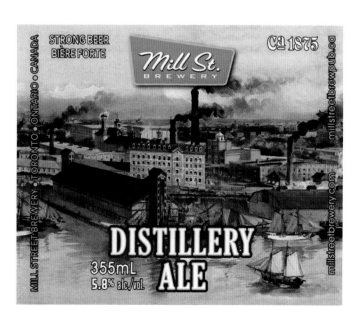

STRONG BEER
BIÈRE FORTE

Ca 1875

Mill St.
BREWERY

MILL STREET BREWERY • TORONTO • ONTARIO • CANADA

millstreetbrewery.com   millstreetbrewpub.ca

DISTILLERY
ALE
355mL
5.8% alc./vol.

GARRISON BREWING COMPANY
Halifax, Nova Scotia

SPRUCE BEER

2015

The year 1997 saw the opening of the Garrison Brewing Company in Halifax; today, it has a permanent home within the Halifax Seaport, a former shipping district that's evolved into a modern, innovative arts and culture hub. Garrison has released a wide range of beers and labels, including seasonals and specialty beers. Their seasonal Spruce Beer is a take on North America's oldest style of beer. The Garrison team picks their own Spruce and Balsam Fir tips and branches.

SPRUCE BEER

Local Spruce & Fir tips from Meander River Farm are combined with Crosbie's blackstrap molasses to re-create North America's oldest beer style. Party like it's 1749!

INGREDIENTS:
Water, Barley Malt, Oats, Spruce & Fir Tips, Molasses, Hops & Yeast

INGRÉDIENTS:
Eau, Malt d'Orge, Avoine, Pousses dÉpinette et de Sapin, Mélasse, Houblon et Levure.

Contains Gluten /
Contient Du Gluten

"At Halifax, spruce beer was the big commodity and thought to be a very good beverage for the men... Brewed for the Conveniency of the Troops it is made of the tops and branches of the spruces-tree, boiled for three hours, then strained into casks... 5 Quarts of Mollaffes will be put into every barrel... as soon as cold, it is fit for use... while encamped at Halifax the soldiers drank great quantities of Spruce Beer... the allowance was three gallons and a half for which he paid seven pence... the Seamen were always fond of drinking Spruce Beer."

Flavoured Strong Ale   Forte Aromatisée

650ml
Produced by /
Produit par

GARRISON
BREWING co
www.garrisonbrewing.com

7.5%
alc./vol.
Halifax NS

2015 VINTAGE
Bottled On: November 25th

6 28432 70112 0

HALF PINTS BREWING COMPANY
Winnipeg, Manitoba

DEAD RINGER

2015

Half Pints Brewing Company, which opened late in 2006, has shown exceptional marketing savvy and connection with its customers, as is evidenced by its successful publicity campaigns. With its roots in small-batch brewing, they used two-litre plastic and now use 341 mL and 650 mL glass bottles. Ever the innovative collaborators, its recent labels have featured unconventional art to promote various styles of beer. The brewery garnered quite a bit of attention when it brewed a limited supply of Queer Beer for the Winnipeg Pride Festival in 2011, and every year since.

STRONG BEER ✕ BIÈRE FORTE

HALF PINTS
BREWING CO.

A complex Belgian style IPA with notes of citrus fruit and cowbell.

CONTAINS:
MALTED BARLEY,
MALTED WHEAT,
HOPS, YEAST,
AND WATER.

650 mL

6.0 % alc./vol.

49 IBU

CRAFT BREWED & BOTTLED BY
HALF PINTS BREWING COMPANY LTD.,
WINNIPEG, MANITOBA, CANADA.
204-832-PINT | HALFPINTSBREWING.COM
KEEP REFRIGERATED.
RETURN FOR REFUND WHERE APPLICABLE.

KELP STOUT

2016

Bryan O'Malley is one of three surfing co-founders of Tofino Brewing Company (established in 2011), which is located in Tofino on the west coast of Vancouver Island, British Columbia. I had the pleasure of visiting the brewery and meeting Bryan in August 2011, and was delighted to find out that his grandfather was William O'Malley of the short-lived Quebec City O'Malley Brewing Company (see page 206). Bryan has a small collection of O'Malley artefacts and was quite surprised to find that I have an O'Malley 24-bottle case and one twelve-ounce. bottle. Today, Tofino makes a wide range of different beers, including this Kelp Stout, which uses kelp harvested from the nearby Pacific Ocean.

KELP STOUT

BREWED & BOTTLED IN TOFINO BRITISH COLUMBIA

TOFINO
BREWING
COMPANY

650 ml

6%
alc/vol

STRONG BEER
ALL NATURAL, UNFILTERED ALE
BIERE FORTE

If there's one sentiment that's constantly repeated among craft beer drinkers it is, "This beer is good but it needs more seaweed!" If we've heard it once, we've heard it a thousand times. Well folks, message received. Tofino Brewing Company presents to you the Kelp Stout. A dark, rich, full-bodied ale brewed with locally harvested Kelp, giving a unique, umami-type quality to this complex beer.

TUFF CITY BREWERY LTD.
C & D – 681 INDUSTRIAL WAY, TOFINO
BRITISH COLUMBIA, V0R 2Z0 CANADA
WWW.TOFINOBREWINGCO.COM

+563064

MOLSON BREWERY
Montreal, Quebec/Toronto, Ontario

1908 HISTORIC PALE ALE

2016

Old beer labels have been reproduced to mark the anniversary of various brands of beer, but rarely can it be said that modern brewers dipped into company archives to create a beer that matches as closely as possible a beer from over 100 years ago.

This beer was released by Molson in January 2016 in both 625 mL bottles and 355 mL bottles, with a distinctive tag on the 625 mL bottles as well. Many breweries today use tags such as this on their bottles and growlers.

NO PRESERVATIVES/SANS AGENTS DE CONSERVATION • UNFILTERED/NON FILTRÉE

JOHN H. R. MOLSON & BROS.

MOLSON'S BREWERY LIMITED SUCCESSORS

TRADE MARK

1908

HISTORIC PALE ALE • PALE ALE HISTORIQUE

625 mL 6.8% alc./vol.

STRONG BEER • BIÈRE FORTE

MONTREAL

©TM/MC MOLSON CANADA 2005 • BREWED IN MONTREAL, CANADA/BRASSÉE À MONTRÉAL, CANADA • UNION MADE/FAB. SYND. • 1-800-MOLSON • 107005

JOHN H. R. MOLSON & BROS.

MONTREAL

1908

HISTORIC PALE ALE • PALE ALE HISTORIQUE

ACKNOWLEDGEMENTS

I was pleasantly surprised last year when Taryn Boyd from TouchWood Editions proposed that we collaborate on a book to illustrate 150 years of Canadian beer labels using the collection of pre-1945 labels I donated to the Fisher Rare Book Library at the University of Toronto in 2011—thanks to the request from Anne Dondertman, then acting director of the Fisher library. I'd also like to express my gratitude to Elizabeth Ridolfo of the Fisher Rare Book Library for her assistance in making many of these rare labels available on the library's website, where they first caught Taryn's attention. Thanks are due as well to Renée Layberry, TouchWood's in-house editor, who provided assistance in putting together the label notes for this book.

I'd like to thank my fellow collectors (brewerianists) for their help in selecting the labels and putting these historical notes in writing. These collectors include Gordon Holder (brewerianacollectors.ca), my long-time "beer buddy" with whom I have visited breweries from St. John's, Newfoundland to Tofino, British Columbia, and all the provinces in between. I have to thank Dave Craig from Winnipeg, Jim Duffy from Toronto (who is in charge of the Label of the Year Awards), Robert Barkwell from Fort Qu'Appelle, and Richard Worsfold from Brampton, for all their help with scouring information.

I must express my appreciation for Loren Newman, publisher of the Canadian Brewerianist Newsletter, who brought together fellow Canadian collectors and wrote about the history of many Canadian breweries, both older and current.

Special thanks must also be paid to the late Richard Sweet, whose historical notes and dates for breweries across Canada have been invaluable in dating many of the labels and the breweries included in this book. Thanks as well to the many current brewers who have helped me build my collection of labels, coasters, business cards, and other mementos from their breweries in all parts of Canada. I must also acknowledge with gratitude my two local pubs: An Sibín Pub and Stout Irish Pub. And, finally, thanks to the staff of the Exchange Loft Computer Room at the Ralph Thornton Centre. I have deeply appreciated their expertise and the use of their equipment while I put together this book.

INDEX

IMAGE PERMISSIONS
These labels have been either scanned from the author's personal collection or provided by the brewery. Many of the early labels are from breweries that have been long out of business. They may have closed as a result of Prohibition, or were bought by another company, or simply closed down.

The publisher and the author extend special thanks to the Thomas Fisher Rare Book Library at the University of Toronto for kindly providing many digital scans. To see more labels donated to the library from the author's collection, visit www.flickr.com/photos/thomasfisherlibrary/albums.

The publisher and author would also like to extend special thanks to the following breweries who kindly supplied images and permission to print their labels:

A l'abri de la Tempete (Anne-Marie Lachance)
Big Rock Brewery (Stuart Karol)
Brasserie Vieux-Montreal (George Fountotos)
Collective Arts Brewing (Jeff Tkachuk and Bob Russell)
Dieu du Ciel! (Leïla Alexandre)
Fort Garry Brewing (Orest Horechko)
Gahan Brewery (Mike Roberts and George MacIntyre)
Garrison Brewing Company (Justin Zinck)
Great Lakes Brewery (Troy Burtch)
Great Western Brewing Company
Half Pints Brewing Co. (David Rudge)
Labatt Breweries (Sharon McKay)
Mano's Grill and Brewhouse (Taso and Louis Barlas)
Mill Street Brewery (Steve Abrams)
Mission Springs Brewing Company (Alexis Knights)
Molson Coors (Lori Ball)
Moosehead Breweries (Suzanne Laughton)
Mt. Begbie Brewery (Tracey Larsen)
Niagara College Teaching Brewery (Steve Gill)
Paddock Wood Brewing Co. (Stephen Cavan)
Phillips Brewing and Malting Company (Matt Lockhart)
Picaroons Traditional Ales (Dennis Goodwin)
Quidi Vidi Brewery (Justin Fong)
Sleeman Breweries (Sue Keuhl)
Steam Whistle Brewing (Chris Johnston)
Tofino Brewing Company (Bryan O'Malley)
Trafalgar Brewing and Distilling (Dave Jamieson)
Yukon Brewing (Bob Baxter)

ADDITIONAL PHOTO CREDITS
Page 275: Jim Duffy
Page 207: Gord Holder

LAWRENCE (LARRY) CARL SHERK was the last Sherk to be born in one of the many Sherk family farmhouses around the village of Sherkston—now part of the town of Port Colborne, Ontario—where he grew up and went to school. From there he went to college in Guelph, post-graduate school at Cornell University, and then spent a year visiting gardens and nurseries in Europe. After several years with Agriculture Canada in Ottawa, he joined the staff of Sheridan Nurseries in Etobicoke, Ontario.

In February 1972, a holiday in San Francisco turned everything upside down when he visited a house where the walls were covered with various kinds of advertising nostalgia and breweriana. Returning to Toronto, he decided to find a few advertising signs to decorate a stairwell. Soon he acquired several beer trays to decorate his kitchen. Then, "all hell broke loose!" as dealers started offering him ashtrays and bottle openers; before long, his passion for collecting Canadian breweriana was in full swing.

Larry's first sixty labels, circa 1890–1910, were acquired in January 1975 when he found an old printer's sample book. He added to this cache by purchasing other labels, and as time went on he added more labels through contacts in breweries spanning from the Atlantic to the Pacific, and by trading with fellow collectors from across Canada.

In 2011, Anne Dondertman, then acting director of the Fisher Rare Books Library at the University of Toronto, convinced Larry to donate the pre-1945 portion of his label collection to the library. Anne went on to have it declared a National Treasure by Heritage Canada, and a large number of labels were scanned and made available for public viewing on the university's website.

Edited by Renée Layberry
Proofread by Claire Philipson
Cover design by Setareh Ashrafologhalai
Interior design by Pete Kohut

LIBRARY AND ARCHIVES CANADA CATALOGUING IN PUBLICATION
Sherk, Lawrence C., author
150 years of Canadian beer labels / Lawrence C. Sherk.

Issued in print and electronic formats.
ISBN 978-1-77151-192-6

1. Beer labels—Canada—History. I. Title. II. Title: One hundred fifty years of Canadian beer labels.

NC1002.B4S54 2016   741.6'92   C2016-904063-1

We acknowledge the financial support of the Government of Canada through the Canada Book Fund (CBF), the Canada Council for the Arts, and of the province of British Columbia through the Book Publishing Tax Credit and the British Columbia Arts Council.

This book was produced using FSC®-certified, acid-free paper, processed chlorine free, and printed with soya-based inks.

PRINTED IN CHINA

20 19 18 17 16   1 2 3 4 5